Cycling San Diego

Revised, Expanded
Third Edition

Nelson Copp • *Jerry Schad*

Sunbelt Publications

Printing History:

FIRST EDITION
First Printing   November 1986
Second Printing February 1987
Third Printing   October 1987
Fourth Printing March 1989

SECOND EDITION
First Printing   January 1992
Second Printing June 1996

THIRD EDITION
First Printing   August 2002

Photos on pages 6, 13, 16, 19, 21, and 51
by Nelson Copp

All other photos by Jerry Schad

Cover design by Mooki Design

Cover photo by Jerry Schad

Library of Congress Cataloging-in-Publication Data

Copp, Nelson.
   Cycling San Diego / by Nelson Copp and Jerry Schad.-- 3rd ed.
     p. cm.
   Includes bibliographical references and index.
     ISBN 0-932653-52-9
     1.   Bicycle touring--California--San Diego County--Guidebooks. 2.   San
   Diego County (Calif.)--Guidebooks. I. Schad, Jerry. II. Title.
     GV1045.5.C22 S257 2002
       796.6'2'09794'98--dc21
                                          2002007756

Manufactured in the United States of America

Published by:
Sunbelt Publications
1250 Fayette Street
El Cajon, CA 92020

Preface

As San Diego County's population approaches the three million mark, it seems as though freeways, housing developments, shopping centers, and industrial complexes have all but strangled our once-serene area.

Rushing from one place to another on the freeway, it's easy to overlook the pleasant neighborhood byways that sometimes lie just beyond the din of traffic. Likewise, we often forget about the miles of quiet backcountry roads lacing the county's vast, sparsely populated interior.

If you can explore these less-traveled byways in a relaxed state of mind, preferably on two wheels, you can rediscover—or maybe discover for the first time—San Diego County's special charms: its unique urban enclaves, its beautiful coastline and bays, its rugged foothills and mountains, and its serene desert spaces.

As an effective aid to doing that, we offer herein a comprehensive selection of trips for cyclists of every level of ability and persuasion. This new edition of *Cycling San Diego* includes more new rides than the previous edition. We've continued the policy of choosing rides that avoid, wherever possible, heavily trafficked roadways. If we do route you along a major road, we at least try to recommend the best direction to take along that road, or recommend the best times of day for avoiding conflicts with car traffic.

We've also made a special effort to devise loop trips—as opposed to out-and-back trips—to take maximum advantage of the scenery. Several trips added in this edition include rough-surfaced dirt roads requiring the use of mountain bikes. Other new trips consist of paved roads along with segments of dirt roads that are usually negotiable by sturdy ten-speeds or hybrid road-mountain bikes.

In the appendices you'll find descriptions of the best ways to pedal out of San Diego County and into adjacent counties. You'll also find a couple of write-ups highlighting multi-day rides around the county's perimeter.

Cycling San Diego will continue to evolve as San Diego County itself grows and changes. We welcome your comments. Please write us in care of Sunbelt Publications, 1250 Fayette Street, El Cajon, CA 92020.

Nelson Copp • Jerry Schad

Publisher's Note

Sunbelt is most pleased to present this third edition of *Cycling San Diego* by well-known co-authors Nelson Copp and Jerry Schad. As the county's largest and most comprehensive guide to road biking and now including many exciting mountain biking routes, it is no wonder that it has been a regional favorite for over fifteen years. This book is a welcome companion to our best-selling San Diego Mountain Bike Guide by Daniel Greenstadt. Although some mountain bike descriptions overlap in the most favored riding areas (e.g., Cuyamaca Rancho State Park, Palomar Mountain area), the two works remain delightfully separate and complementary with very different styles of writing, maps, trip presentations, and background information. With both of these books by the most qualified author-cyclists of our region, riders can enjoy many years of healthy and exciting exploration on the roads and trails of "America's Finest County."

Lowell Lindsay

Contents

Urban and Coastal Rides

Rural and Foothill Rides

Mountain and Desert Rides

Trip No.

*Lunchtime or after work ride

County Line at Pala Road

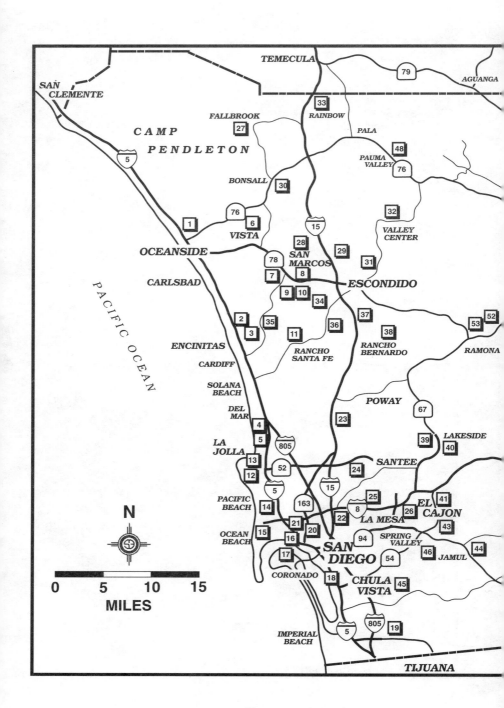

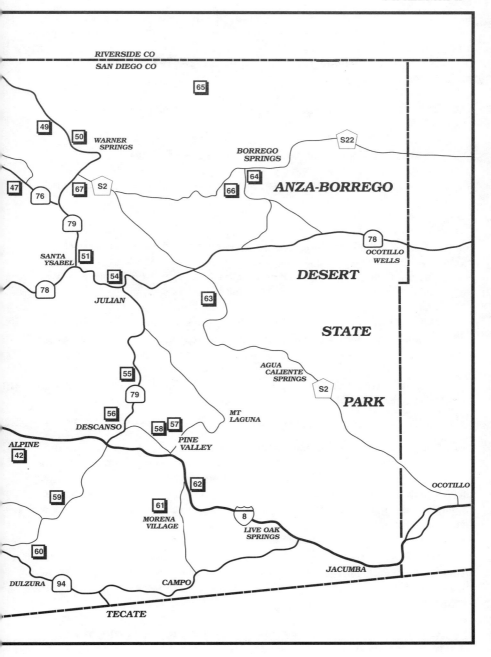

How to Use This Book

Each of the 67 sequentially numbered trips in this book follows a consistent format. To locate the starting point of each trip with respect to major highways and cities, first glance at the area map of San Diego County in the front of the book. The numbers in shadow boxes refer to the starting points of each numbered trip.

Each trip description includes a capsulized summary of information that may be useful for ride selection.

The **Distance** figure refers to the total distance of the route as described in the text and plotted on the accompanying trip map and elevation profile. A look at that map usually reveals ways in which the trip might be shortened or extended, should you wish to customize your trip.

Elevation Gain refers to the total (not net) amount of elevation gained during the trip. For a loop trip, this refers to the sum of all the elevation gains, and equivalently the sum of all the elevation losses. For an out-and-back trip, this refers to the total gain of both the out and the back segments. For a one-way trip, both total gain and total loss figures are given.

Riding Time is an estimated figure to be used for comparative purposes. Fast riders may be able to complete the trip non-stop in perhaps half the time, while leisurely riders may take 50 percent more time than that stated.

The **Difficulty** rating is also relative. One-star rides (*) are easy, two-star rides (**) are moderate, three star rides (***) are moderately strenuous, and four-star rides (****) are strenuous.

Arrows are included on the trip maps to assist you in tracing each route, which begins and ends at a boxed number. (For point-to-point trips there are two identical boxed numbers for the start and end points.) Several of the trip maps include more than one trip. In those cases, let the boxed numbers be your way of finding the starting point for a given trip (you may have to go forward or back a few pages to find the right map).

Bike paths, or routes on which bicycles are entirely separated from auto traffic, are indicated on our maps by dashed lines. These maps can be supplemented by maps available from other sources. See Appendix 4—Resources and Recommended Reading.

All trips with a substantial amount of elevation gain—generally more than 1000 feet—have an elevation profile included. Each profile is based on the route as described in the text and indicated by arrows on the map. The profiles are vertically exaggerated to better illustrate the rise and fall of the route, but are accurate with respect to the elevation and distance scales given.

IMPORTANT NOTE: Although space in this book does not permit us to fully discuss bicycle preparedness and safe riding practices, we want to emphasize the following:

- Always wear a hard-shell helmet when bicycling.
- The more remote trips in this book traverse areas where water may be scarce or unavailable; carry a water bottle (or two) on the longer rides.
- On the longer rides, carry a lunch or bring money to purchase food along the way.
- Carry a patch kit, a simple repair kit, and a tire pump. An extra inner tube can also be handy. Flat tires can and do happen in remote areas!
- Wear sun-protective clothing and sunscreen on bright, sunny days; and wear warm clothing for chilly mornings and evenings. San Diego County's inland areas especially tend to experience wide swings in temperature.

SPECIAL NOTE FOR MOUNTAIN BIKERS: Travel on a mountain bike often permits easy access to areas of the outdoors formerly accessible only by foot or horse. But mountain bikes are not welcome everywhere. In California state parks they are usually restricted to certain dirt roads. On national forest lands they usually aren't restricted, except on the Pacific Crest Trail. Mountain bikers are banned from the 100+ miles of the PCT in San Diego County and also in all officially designated wilderness areas. In this book, our mountain-bike trips route you mostly over dirt roads that are also open to automobile traffic. Nevertheless, here are some guidelines for those of you who may feel the call of the wild and be tempted to turn off the beaten path:

- Never ride cross-country or create your own trail.
- Make certain the trail you want to ride is legally open to bicycling.
- Don't ride trails that cannot withstand erosion cause by tire tracks. Never cut switchbacks. Avoid muddy trails—wait until the surface dries and becomes firm.
- Always yield the right of way to hikers and horseback riders even if you have to stop and dismount.
- Control your speed at all times (many parks have a 15 mph speed limit for bikes).
- Approach other trail users slowly. Let others know of your presence. Slow down when you approach switchbacks and blind curves (this is where conflict with others often occurs).

Trip 1. Camp Pendleton Coast

Starting Point: Oceanside
GPS: Lat/Long 33° 12′ 38″, 117° 23′ 4″;
UTM 11S 464159mE 3674504mN
Distance: 40 miles (round trip)
Elevation Gain: 1100 feet
Riding Time: 3.5 hours
Road Conditions: Smooth roads with wide shoulders; bike paths (bumpy in places)
Traffic Conditions: Light to moderate on roads; no motorized traffic on bike paths
Difficulty: ***
Equipment: Any multi-geared bike

Surf, sand, picturesque bluffs, and rolling hills. Salty breezes and the ever-present licorice scent of wild fennel. The rhythmic bumping of your tires over the pavement of an old four-lane highway abandoned save for the occasional lizard or snake that may cross your path. This and more await you on one of the flatter and easier bike rides in North San Diego County: the coastal route through Camp Pendleton.

The Camp Pendleton route is the cyclist's only alternative to the 17-mile stretch of Interstate 5 between Oceanside and San Clemente. It's also an important link in the main Pacific coast route followed in its entirety by hundreds of riders yearly. You'll be routed over Marine-base access roads, abandoned sections of the old U.S. Highway 101, and short sections of bike path. Do not veer off of the designated bike route.

During most periods of fair weather, winds tend to come from the southwest before about 10 a.m. and from the northwest thereafter. An early start from Oceanside will allow you to take advantage of these winds, as well as cooler temperatures. Make sure you're finished by sunset; the base closes for bike riders at dusk.

If you arrive in Oceanside by car, take the Oceanside Harbor Drive/Camp Pendleton exit off Interstate 5, turn right on San Rafael Drive (just shy of the main Camp Pendleton gate), and park in the residential area beyond the red-painted curbs. This is our assumed starting point. If you're arriving by pedal power from Oceanside's main drag—Hill Street— use Oceanside Harbor Drive to cross I-5 and approach the gate directly.

Camp Pendleton is sometimes closed to cyclists due to heightened security measures, in which case you will need to ride on Interstate 5. Enter the freeway before reaching the main gate. Exit at Las Pulgas Road and turn left on an abandoned section of Highway 101 just before the railroad undercrossing. When you pull up to the main gate on your bicycle, be prepared to show your driver's license or a valid ID. Go straight ahead past the gate on Vandegrift Boulevard for 1.5 miles, and make a left turn at the traffic light, Stuart Mesa Road. Heading north now, you cross the Santa Margarita River and climb a half-mile-long incline to reach Stuart Mesa. Along the road ahead, you'll see everything from flower fields and row crops (on land leased to growers) to military complexes, including camouflaged encampments. On some days, tanks lumber across the scrubby land by the roadside, and helicopters practice maneuvers overhead.

After a total of about nine miles, a cluster of refurbished ranch buildings (used by Boy Scouts) comes into view on the left. There you turn left on Las Pulgas Road and pedal up and over a small hill toward I-5. Just beyond the railroad undercrossing, but before the I-5 ramps, go right onto a section of the abandoned Highway 101 roadbed (the ride picks up here if you rode on Interstate 5). After 1.5 miles you veer left, pass through a tunnel under the freeway, and pick up another piece of the old highway that fronts the seaside bluffs.

The south boundary of San Onofre State beach is next: you may have to dismount to get past the vehicle-blocking poles. The blufftop and beachfront property ahead is leased from the Marine Corps by the state. In the next 3.5 miles, the old highway serves as parking and camping space for beach visitors. Unlike those arriving by car, you pay nothing for the privilege of passing through on a bike. A number of short trails descend from the bluffs to the beach below—all are good diversions if you can secure your bike topside.

Beyond the main entrance to the state beach, past the San Onofre Nuclear Generating Station, you'll come to the final link of bikeway leading to San Clemente. Make a sharp left turn onto a paved bikeway just before the road veers right to pass over I-5. This bikeway passes over San Mateo Creek, where you can follow a 0.3-mile-long paved path on the left to reach Trestles Beach, a well-known surfing spot. The main path continues uphill to a frontage road along I-5 at the south edge of San Clemente. A pedestrian entrance to San Clemente State Beach park—a good place for picnicking—lies a short mile ahead on the west frontage road of I-5. At either destination, you can have lunch, relax, and let the usual late-morning and afternoon tailwind come up before you head back to Oceanside.

Trip 1

Stuart Mesa Road

Trip 2. South Carlsbad Loop

Starting Point: North Encinitas
GPS: Lat/Long 33° 4′ 57″, 117° 18′ 29″;
UTM 11S 471248mE 3660271mN
Distance: 16 miles
Elevation Gain: 850 feet
Riding Time: 2 hours
Road Conditions: Smooth, paved roads with narrow to wide shoulders
Traffic Conditions: Moderate
Difficulty: **
Equipment: Any multi-geared bike

New suburban arterial streets in south Carlsbad and north Encinitas—nearly every one striped with bicycle lanes—invite you to take a spin on two skinny wheels. The looping route described here is a beautiful Sunday early-morning ride, especially in the winter, when the morning sun spills over the mountains to the east and the hushed air retains the chill of the night.

Park near the intersection of La Costa Avenue and Coast (Old) Highway 101 in northernmost Encinitas. Roll north on the coast highway (which becomes Carlsbad Boulevard) down past South Carlsbad State Beach.

When your reach Poinsettia Lane at 1.4 miles, turn right, pass over Interstate 5, and turn right at Batiquitos Drive, 2.2 miles into your ride. Roll down and up several times on Batiquitos, flanked by new houses, passing various access points to the Batiquitos Lagoon shoreline on the right (bicycles are not permitted on the shoreline trail.) At 4.6 miles, you reach Aviara Parkway. Turn right there and right again at El Camino Real, a major intersection at 5.4 miles. Swoop down out of the suburbs and into a patch of open space fronting Batiquitos

Lagoon. Before La Costa Avenue, you pass over San Marcos Creek that winds its way through the nearby hills from Lake San Marcos and beyond.

At 6.6 miles you'll make a left at La Costa Avenue (major intersection) and start a long climb up into the coastal hills. When your reach Rancho Santa Fe Road turn right, and continue to Calle Barcelona on the right.

Follow the gentle curves of nearly traffic-free Calle Barcelona through the new housing development, La Costa Valley, and arrive back at El Camino Real, 10.8 miles. Make a left there, glide a short way over to the next intersection (Olivenhain Road on the left, Leucadia Boulevard on the right), and turn right. The brand-new section of Leucadia Boulevard on the right swoops uphill and crosses Encinitas Ranch Golf Course. Make a right just past the golf course on Quail Gardens Drive. Pedal north on this serene, narrow thoroughfare, enjoying near and distant views of newer and older housing developments covering the coastal hills. Quail Gardens Drive soon pitches downhill on a long, wide curve; make no turns as its name changes to Quail Hollow Drive.

Quail Hollow Drive ends at Saxony Road. Turn right and finish the downhill run to La Costa Avenue (14.4 miles). Follow La Costa Avenue west, back to the coast highway in Encinitas, clocking in at just under 16 miles for the loop you've covered.

Options: To lengthen the ride another four miles and see more of the coastline, continue straight on Carlsbad Boulevard instead of turning right on Poinsettia Lane. Turn right on Palomar Airport Road, ride inland for 3.7 miles, then go right (south) on El Camino Real.

Trip 2

Trip 3. La Costa Valley

Starting Point: La Costa (Carlsbad)
GPS: Lat/Long 33° 4′ 32″, 117° 15′ 35″;
UTM 11S 475761mE 3659488mN
Distance: 4 miles
Elevation Gain: 100 feet
Riding Time: 1 hour
Road Conditions: Smooth dirt trails,
smooth pavement
Traffic Conditions: Light
Difficulty: *
Equipment: Any multi-geared bike

Carlsbad, known as the "Village by the Sea," is something of an anachronism. It boasts a world-class business environment, two world-class resorts and golf courses, and a theme park, but yet sets aside 40 percent of its land for open space. This short ride with several options will provide a glimpse of some of

that open space in the La Costa Valley master planned community. Opened in April 1998, La Costa Valley set aside some 100 plus acres of recreation and preserved open space amongst the houses to provide recreational areas and habitat links to other nearby areas.

Founded during the land boom of 1880s, Carlsbad was named for a famous spa in Karlsbad, Bohemia, whose waters were identical to those found in a local mineral well. The water became famous for its healing powers. Later known as the Avocado Capital of the World, Carlsbad was an agricultural community for years. Carlsbad, incorporated as a city in 1952, has grown substantially since then.

Trip 3

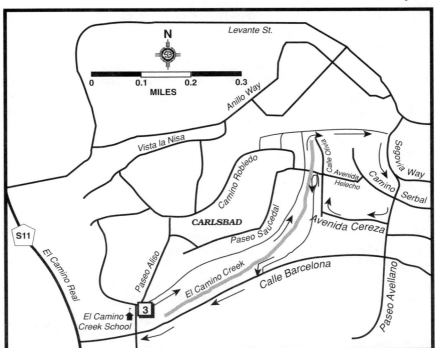

La Costa Valley

To start the ride, park near El Camino Creek Elementary School on Paseo Aliso just west of Calle Barcelona near the junction of El Camino Real and Olivenhain Road. Across from the school trail markers with the distinctive La Costa Valley logo—a sunrise over fields, mark the beginning of the trail system. Head east on this smooth dirt trail as it follows the contours up the valley alongside the La Costa Valley wetlands. Most of the riparian vegetation is native including sycamore trees, willows, lemonade berry, and ceanothus. It also provides a habitat for many animals such as rabbits and coyotes. We saw several rabbits on our ride. To make a short loop, follow the sidewalk right at Avenida Helecho a few feet then turn right on the paved trail that follows the south side of the creek. When you reach Calle Barcelona, turn right, then right again on Paseo Aliso to return to your starting point.

To explore further, cross Avenida Helecho and follow the trail as it climbs then drops down to a T-junction. Left takes you up a small hill behind a row of houses that exits onto Camino Robledo in two places. Our recommended route is right, where you drop down to a small creek bed built up with gravel and bordered by boulders to prevent erosion. Continue up the steep hill that thankfully flattens out before it reaches Segovia Way. Turn right and pass by the newest part of the development in the valley. Turn right on Paseo Avellano and then right on Avenida Cereza which quickly drops to Calle Olivia. Turn right, then left on Avenida Helecho to find the paved trail on the south side of the creek. Turn left there to make your way back to Calle Barcelona where a right, then right again on Paseo Aliso ends the ride.

Options: After reaching Segovia Way, you can turn left to Levante Street for an exhilarating downhill run to El Camino Real. Turn left then left again on Calle Barcelona to return to La Costa Valley.

Trip 4. North County Coast

Starting Point: Solana Beach
GPS: Lat/Long 32° 59′ 29″, 117° 16′ 21″;
UTM 11S 474544mE 3650188mN
Distance: 43 miles
Elevation Gain: 800 feet
Riding Time: 4 hours
Road Conditions: Smooth roads with narrow to wide shoulders
Traffic Conditions: Light on back roads and streets; moderate to heavy on the old coast highway, where bike lanes provide some protection
Difficulty: ***
Equipment: Any multi-geared bike

San Diego's North County coastline attracts a growing stream of cyclists intent on enjoying the almost-constant fresh breezes blowing off the ocean. Traffic can be quite heavy on the old coast highway, however. This ride offers several alternative detours that will keep you off the busy coastal route, and lets you explore some of the better back roads and quiet streets. Feel free to add or drop parts of this ride if you want to change the length.

You can start just about anywhere, but we suggest Solana Beach since parking is readily available there. Exit Interstate 5 at Lomas Santa Fe Drive and head west toward the coast. Plenty of parking is available on Sierra Avenue near Fletcher Cove Park.

Start cycling south on Sierra Avenue. Turn left at the end of the street on Border Avenue and then quickly right on Old Highway 101. This old road, now known in the various coastal towns as Camino Del Mar, North Torrey Pines Road, and Carlsbad Boulevard, was relieved of its role as a major highway when Interstate 5 was completed in the 1960s. As you head downhill toward Del Mar, North Bluff Preserve is on your right and the

Del Mar Racetrack and county fairgrounds are on your left. You'll cross the tidal channel of the San Dieguito River as you enter Del Mar. At 1.7 miles, veer right on Coast Boulevard and continue south past the old Del Mar Amtrak station and the recently refurbished Powerhouse Building. Built to provide the original Stratford Inn with electricity and hot water, the powerhouse provided electricity for all of Del Mar until 1918. It was acquired with the surrounding park area in 1983 by the City of Del Mar and transformed into a multi-purpose building. Seagrove Park, overlooking the ocean on the right, is one of San Diego's hidden treasures—it's a good spot for filling your water bottle.

Continue south on what is now Ocean Avenue to the **T**-intersection with unmarked 13th Street. Go left there, right on Stratford Court, right on 12th, and then left on Stratford Court to resume your southward journey. You're seeing some of the best of "old" Del Mar, graced with mature trees and landscaping. Del Mar residents jealously guard their streets and properties against the kind of wholesale development now taking place over the hills to the east.

Watch for a side street named "Little Orphan Alley" between 7th and 8th streets. Continue straight into Del Mar Woods and ride onto the small concrete sidewalk signed BIKE ROUTE at 3.5 miles. This little-known route soon joins Camino Del Mar, which now begins to glide down to Torrey Pines State Beach. Take in the fabulous view of the Torrey Pines cliffs and the La Jolla coastline ahead.

Although it requires a burst of short-term strength, the so-called "inside

Trip 4

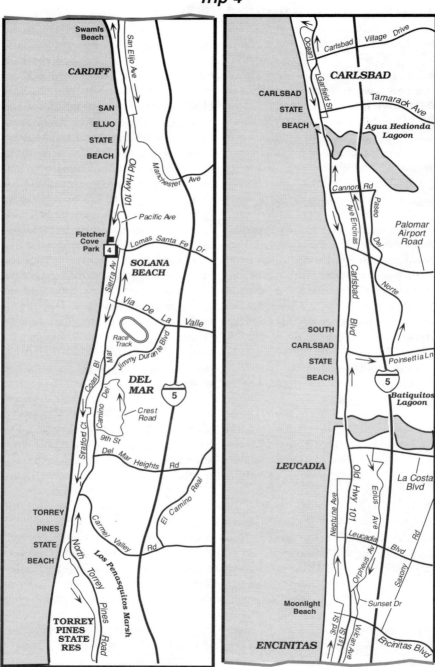

South half   **North half**

route" up through Torrey Pines State Reserve adds a scenic dimension. Veer right at the entrance to Torrey Pines State Beach and tackle the steep road climbing into the reserve. The reserve itself is unique in that it is only one of two places on earth where Torrey pines grow in their native habitat. The museum at the crest of the hill is well worth a visit. Continue riding past the museum (restrooms and water are available on your right), walk your bike past a gate, and cross North Torrey Pines Road at the traffic light on Torrey Pines Science Park North.

Head north now on North Torrey Pines Road, and soon you'll be heading down the "outside route" back to Torrey Pines State Beach. You can look down on the Los Penasquitos tidal marsh area as you effortlessly lose about 300 feet of elevation. Climb the hill back into Del Mar. You could continue straight through Del Mar on Camino Del Mar, but for more challenge and fun, follow the circuitous side tour on the hillside to the east as described below.

Turn right on 9th Street, and then right on Highland Avenue. Highland becomes Hoska Drive. Continue climbing until you reach Crest Road. Turn left and follow Crest. Soon you're riding along the top of a ridge, and there's a great view northeast into the San Dieguito River Valley. At a circular roundabout, turn right onto Avenida Primavera. Look for the unique "Del Mar Castle" on the right. Continue straight onto Serpentine Drive. True to its name, Serpentine winds its way downhill. Watch your speed on all these narrow, windy roads. Turn right on Forest Way, and right on Zapo Street. Then turn left on Bellaire Street and left again on Sea View Avenue. The view of the ocean is striking from this vantage

Los Peñasquitos Marsh

point. Sea View then drops back to Camino Del Mar, where you turn right.

Ahead on Camino Del Mar, you'll need to bear left to stay on it. Cross the San Dieguito River again and climb the short hill into Solana Beach. When you reach Lomas Santa Fe Drive you can turn left to return to your starting point and end the ride at 13.3 miles if you want to cut it short.

To continue north, pedal past Cardiff State Beach and the San Elijo Lagoon County Park and Ecological Reserve. This lagoon and several others you'll see

ahead are valuable as hatcheries and feeding areas for fish and waterfowl. Coastal lagoons and wetlands like these are becoming more and more rare as the demand for land use increases.

Swami's, the local name for the beach just below the imposing Self-Realization Fellowship Temple, is on your left as you enter Encinitas. Turn left at the stop sign on J Street, then right on 3rd Street. Most of the streets, H through C, have beach overlooks for sampling the view. Watch for the unique "houseboats"—the SS Moonlight and SS Encinitas—on your left. Blast down the steep hill that crosses Encinitas Boulevard and then up the other side. Curve left onto Sylvia Street and then right onto Neptune Avenue. Neptune soon becomes one-way northbound. Beacon's, a popular surfing beach, will be on your left as you pedal this quiet street. Turn right on Grandview, and then carefully cross Old Highway 101 and continue north.

Batiquitos Lagoon will be on your right, and South Carlsbad State Beach on your left as you head north into Carlsbad. You may continue straight into Carlsbad, but it's more interesting to take a side route at this point by turning right on Poinsettia Lane. Cross I-5 and then turn left on Paseo Del Norte. This wide road passes through a quiet part of South Carlsbad.

Turn left on Palomar Airport Road, cross I-5 again, and then turn right on Avenida Encinas. Turn left on Cannon Road, then right at Cannon Park onto Carlsbad Boulevard. The Encina power plant monopolizes the view to your right, but keep your eyes left to enjoy Carlsbad State Beach. After passing Agua Hedionda Lagoon, turn right on Sequoia

Avenue and climb a short hill to Garfield Street. Turn left on Garfield and continue to Pine Avenue. Make a right on Pine, then an immediate left on Lincoln Street. Lincoln leads you directly to Carlsbad Boulevard. Continue straight past Magee Park and the Army and Navy Academy—"Home of the Warriors."

Just before the bridge at the north end of Carlsbad, turn left on Mountain View Drive and follow it west until it turns into Ocean Street. Continue south on Ocean back to Carlsbad Boulevard and turn right. After going south another five miles (and passing South Carlsbad State Beach again), turn left on La Costa Boulevard for yet another worthwhile side route.

Take the second right off La Costa Avenue onto Sheridan Road and pass by several greenhouses where impatiens, coleus, and fuchsias are grown. Make a left on Andrew Drive and follow it up the hill, then stay left onto Eolus Avenue. Turn left on Leucadia Boulevard, then quickly jog right onto Orpheus Avenue. As you enjoy the downhill stretch on Orpheus, watch for Sunset Drive on your left. Turn left on Sunset, climb a small hill then continue downhill to Vulcan Avenue. Turn left on Vulcan (it becomes San Elijo Avenue) and continue straight until you reach Chesterfield Drive. Turn right on Chesterfield, then left onto 1st Street (Old Highway 101). Climb the short hill into Solana Beach and turn right on Ocean Street. Finally, turn left on Pacific Avenue and follow it back to your starting point. If you have followed every kink and turn in our description, you've now traveled 43 miles.

Trip 5. Solana Beach Tour

Starting Point: Solana Beach
GPS: Lat/long 32° 59' 29", 117° 16' 21";
UTM 11S 474544mE 3650188mN
Distance: 10 miles
Elevation Gain: 800 feet
Riding Time: 1.5 hours
Road Conditions: Smooth, paved roads with narrow to wide shoulders
Traffic Conditions: Moderate
Difficulty: **
Equipment: Any multi-geared bike

Prior to 1923, the area that is now the city of Solana Beach was known as Lockwood Mesa, and was used for the growing of grains and lima beans. Fletcher Cove, the main public access to the beach, and site of annual community festivals, was created by using a combination of hydraulic washing from Lake Hodges runoff water and extensive steam shovel work that made a gap in the picturesque bluffs. Interstate 5 was originally planned to follow the route of

Coast Highway through this area. Solana Beach officials started lobbying to move it eastward in the late 1940s and in 1957 the state announced that it had selected an uninhabited inland route for Interstate 5. This freeway now bisects Solana Beach inland.

To get a feel for the Solana Beach area, follow this tour through the back streets and hills of Solana Beach. If you time your ride right, you can visit the weekly Solana Beach Farmers' Market on Sunday from 2:00 to 5:00 p.m. for an assortment of farm fresh flowers, baked goods and produce. The market is located across from the Solana Beach train station at Lomas Santa Fe and Cedros Avenue.

Park by Fletcher Cove Beach Park near Lomas Santa Fe Drive and North Coast Highway 101. Turn left on North Sierra Avenue and pedal along a palm tree-lined street. Turn right on Cliff Street

Trip 5

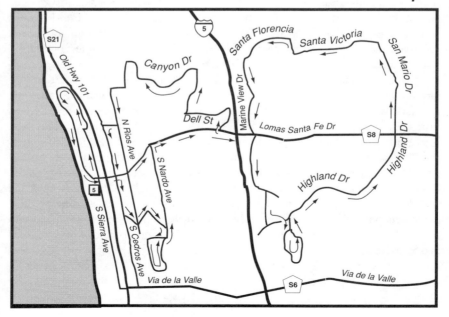

Solana Beach

then left on Acacia Avenue. Look right to see nice views of San Elijo Lagoon. Curve left onto Circle Drive which becomes Pacific Avenue and heads south along the crest of the hill above the beach.

At the bottom of the hill, turn left onto Lomas Santa Fe Drive. Follow it east and turn right on South Cedros Avenue. Pass underneath the big arch proclaiming the recently renovated Cedros Design District. Interesting shops line the street.

At the stop sign, turn left on Rosa Street, then left on Palmitas Street and right on Lirio Street to complete a W-shaped climb up the ridge above the Design District. At South Nardo turn right then right again on Solana Circle West. As you circle through the Park Del Mar neighborhood you are rewarded with great views of Del Mar Beach, the James Scripps Bluff Preserve and the Del Mar Racetrack. Once back at South Nardo Avenue turn left.

Turn right on Lomas Santa Fe Drive and pass under Interstate 5. Note that this area is no longer uninhabited as when the Interstate 5 route was first planned

in the 1950s. Turn right on Marine View Avenue. Follow Marine View to its end and a small turnaround that provides a bird's eye view towards the Del Mar Racetrack. Double back and turn right on Highland Drive and start climbing up the next ridge inland.

Turn right on Avocado Place then right again as Avocado Place loops around the hill. You cruise down a narrow road and then start climbing with a great view eastward to the San Dieguito River Valley. Curve left at the top of the hill and follow Avocado Place back to Highland Drive where you turn right.

Cross Lomas Santa Fe Drive and pass by the upper section of San Dieguito County Park. Turn left on San Mario Drive, then left on Petra Drive. At Santa Victoria turn left and climb the short steep hill in front of you. If you are feeling adventurous, turn right on Santa Helena and quickly drop down to an entrance to the hiking trails and nice view of the San Elijo Lagoon County Park and Ecological Reserve (bicycles are not allowed in the reserve.)

Back on Santa Victoria, turn right on Santa Carina at the Solana Vista School. As you drop quickly down this street turn left on Santa Rosita for an easy way back to Santa Helena Street. If you feel like doing some hills, drop all the way to the bottom and another entrance and nice view into the ecological reserve. Turn left on Santa Queta, right on Santa Hidalga and follow it steeply uphill to Santa Helena.

Turn right on Santa Helena and swoop down to Lomas Santa Fe Drive. Cross under Interstate 5 and take the first right on Solana Hills Drive. Turn left on Dell Street, cross over a couple of "speed humps," then turn right on Glencrest Drive.

Turn left on Canyon Drive and keep an eye out for the beautiful view of the ocean and Solana Beach as the road heads quickly downhill. Stay right when you meet Mar Vista Drive and follow the curve around to an unmarked side street, Holmwood Lane, where you turn right, just past Rawl Place. Turn right on Granados Avenue and follow the sweeping left turn as it turns into Barbara Avenue.

Turn right on Patty Hill Drive then right on North Rios Avenue. Follow it to the end for another nice view and hiking entrance into the ecological reserve. Retrace your route and turn right on Seabright Lane, and right on East Cliff Street (you were on the western extension of Cliff Street earlier in the ride.) Turn left on North Cedros Avenue, pass by the train station, then turn right on Lomas Santa Fe Drive to return to your starting point.

Trip 6. North River - Guajome Loop

Starting Point: Oceanside
GPS: Lat/Long 33° 14′ 53″, 117° 16′ 24″;
UTM 11S 474547mE 3678624mN
Distance: 10 miles
Elevation Gain: 120 feet
Riding Time: 1.5 hours
Road Conditions: Smooth, paved roads with narrow to wide shoulders
Traffic Conditions: Light to moderate
Difficulty: *
Equipment: Any bicycle

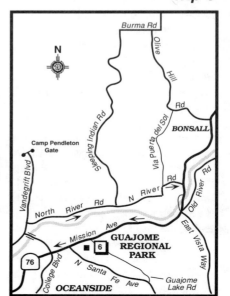

In a region of little rain, even sluggishly flowing rivers are a real treasure. The San Luis Rey River, which flows along the foot of Palomar Mountain and winds it way to the Pacific Ocean at Oceanside, appears nearly dry most of the year. Yet even during intense drought, its steady underground flow nourishes willows, cattails, and the other water-loving plants generally known as riparian vegetation. Less than one half of one percent of San Diego's land area is covered by such vegetation. This ride takes you along a portion of the San Luis Rey River, about 10 miles inland from its mouth near Oceanside Harbor.

To reach the starting point, Guajome Regional Park on Oceanside's inland edge, take Highway 76 (Mission Avenue) 6.5 miles east from Interstate 5, or take the same highway 8.9 miles west from Interstate 15. Turn south on Guajome Lake Road to reach the park entrance. There's a nominal charge for leaving your car inside the park; ample free parking is also available near the entrance.

Cycle back out to busy Highway 76 and head west about a mile to College Boulevard. On your left is Guajome Lake, a tranquil oasis in the midst of the rapidly expanding suburbs. New housing developments are quickly gobbling up the remaining farmland in the area.

Turn right at College Boulevard and cycle on to the bridge over the San Luis Rey River. On the other side, turn right on North River Road. Just a bit farther, you'll have to turn right again to stay on North River Road. The road narrows as houses give way to nut trees and row crops and you sidle up to the north river bank. The sweet smell of anise permeates the air. Soon it will be hard to believe the city is only a few minutes away.

At mile 4.2, Sleeping Indian Road intersects from the left. A side trip north from this point leads into citrus and avocado country—see Options below. Continue east on North River Road, passing Via Puerta del Sol on the left. When you reach Highway 76, turn right, ride south for 0.3 mile, then turn right again on Holly Lane and immediately left on Old Mission Road. Cross over the San Luis Rey River on the old narrow bridge that until recently was the terror of both cyclists and automobile drivers. Thankfully the old bridge was left for cyclists and pedestrians after the new one was finished in 1990. Pedal back up to Highway 76, and rejoin it for the last 2.3 miles back to Guajome Park.

Options: For a longer ride (19 miles total) with plenty of hills, turn north from North River Road onto Sleeping Indian Road. Colorful bougainvillea drape the fences bordering the road for a short while. Then you climb through fragrant citrus groves. A steep, 0.5-mile-long hill takes you into the Morro Hills, with a great view south and west into Vista and Oceanside.

Turn right on Burma Road, and right again on Olive Hill Road. A downhill stretch, past expensive homes, takes you down to Bonsall Pond on the left. Go right on Via Puerta del Sol and ride a 0.6 mile stretch of dirt road (probably soon to be paved). Pavement resumes, and you continue down to North River Road, where you rejoin the route described above.

Trip 7. Vista Loop

Starting Point: Vista
GPS: Lat/Long 33° 9′ 53″, 117° 12′ 57″;
UTM 11S 479862mE 3669374mN
Distance: 25 miles
Elevation Gain: 900 feet
Riding Time: 2 hours
Road Conditions: Smooth, paved roads
with narrow to wide shoulders
Traffic Conditions: Moderate
Difficulty: **
Equipment: Any multi-geared bike

Vista, incorporated in 1963, derives its name from the Spanish word for "view." Vista is nestled amidst colorful hills and valleys in the ever-expanding North San Diego County. This ride will pass in and out of Vista several times as you wind your way along colorful two-lane roads that will remind you of Vista's agricultural roots. This route makes a wonderful early morning ride when the air is quiet and the sounds and smells of occasional fields and farms waft their way to you.

Park near the intersection of Shadowridge Drive and Sycamore Avenue just south of Highway 78. Head west on Shadowridge Drive and roll uphill past the Shadowridge Golf Course. This section of road was a favorite ending for the Tour de North County ride that used to wind through many parts of Vista. When you reach Melrose Drive at 1.6 miles, turn right. As you pass Buena Vista High School on your left, turn right on Live Oak Road.

Turn left on Lupine Hills Drive and begin a moderate climb. After cresting the high point, you will fly down the other side past Thibodo Park. Keep an eye out for Chaparral Drive where you turn left, then left again on Thibodo Road. You will parallel Highway 78 as you climb to the crest and turn left on Mar Vista Drive. Mar Vista was recently paved and the twisting downhill run passes orchards, nurseries, and an occasional rooster crowing.

Vista Loop

Turn right on Buena Vista Drive then left on Sunset Drive. The next mile or so will take you back 10 to 20 years as you climb up, down, and past farms and open spaces on a narrow two-lane road. As you pass Ridge Drive, take in the nice views of Vista surrounding you. At 8.2 miles, cross over Highway 78 where the road changes to Emerald Drive. Past Olive Avenue, Emerald starts down a wonderful hill and changes its name again to North Avenue. You parallel railroad tracks and Alta Creek on your left.

Turn left on Temple Heights Drive and follow it across the railroad tracks and then Oceanside Boulevard. Temple Heights slowly climbs the ridge in front of you and eventually continues west along the ridge. The road splits into a delightful two-lane tree-lined thoroughfare and then drops you down to College Boulevard.

Turn right at College Boulevard, then right again at Mesa Drive. Rancho Del Oro Community Park is on your right if you want to stop and take a break. Mesa is a wonderful downhill run that brings you to North Santa Fe Avenue. Turn right and pass by Guajome Regional Park on your left. The Welcome to Historic Vista sign indicates you are close to the old Rancho Guajome Adobe (tours available at certain times). Turn left on Osborne Street. On Osborne Street, you leave the busy road behind and pass by colorful flowers and nurseries, including one that specializes in orchids and carnivorous plants. The threat of construction at the corner of Osborne Street may change the quiet nature of this area in the future.

At 18 miles, turn right on East Vista Way and climb to East Warmlands Avenue where you will turn left. At the top of a short hill, curve right to stay on Warmlands. This rolling road offers views of Vista and the surrounding hills and takes you by eucalyptus, orange, avocado, and jacaranda trees, and colorful oleander bushes.

Turn left at Foothill Drive and stay right when it passes San Clemente Avenue. At 22.6 miles, turn left on Vista Drive. At Buena Creek Road, turn right and blast along this winding stretch of road that follows the path of Buena Creek. Turn right at South Santa Fe Avenue and then a quick left on Robelini Drive. The recent addition of North County Square removed some of the fun curves in Robelini. Robelini turns into Sycamore Avenue and passes under Highway 78, returning to your starting point.

Options: To extend the ride to 41 miles, you could turn left on North Santa Fe Avenue after Mesa Drive, left on Mission Avenue, then right on College Boulevard. Turn right on Vandegrift Boulevard then right again on North River Road (see the North River-Guajome Loop ride for a description of this area.) Turn left on Mission Road (Highway 76) then right on Camino Del Rey. After passing under Highway 15, turn right on Old Highway 395 that turns into Champagne Boulevard. Turn right on Deer Springs Road, then right on Buena Creek Road. Jog right on South Santa Fe Avenue then left on Robelini Drive to end the ride.

Trip 8. San Marcos Loop

Starting Point: San Marcos
GPS Lat/Long 33° 8′ 50″, 117° 7′ 56″;
UTM 11S 487681mE 3667435mN
Distance: 25 miles
Elevation Gain: 500 feet
Riding Time: 2 hours
Road Conditions: Smooth, paved roads
with narrow to wide shoulders
Traffic Conditions: Moderate
Difficulty: **
Equipment: Any multi-geared bike

Sandwiched between Carlsbad and
Escondido, San Marcos manages to
maintain its unique character of having
once been part of a large Mexican rancho. In fact, a large part of the agricultural industry in North County is still
harvested here. This ride takes you
through the hills and areas surrounding
San Marcos and provides a glimpse of
both the growing city and its pockets of
agriculture.

Park near Woodland Park, off of
Highway 78 and Woodland Parkway in
San Marcos. This is also a nice place to
relax and have a snack after the ride.
Begin by heading south on Woodland

Parkway and cross under Highway 78.
Turn right on Barham Drive, then left at
Twin Oaks Valley Road. California State
University at San Marcos, founded in
1989, is on your left.

Turn right on Craven Road—it is flat
for a short distance and then begins a nice
downhill run. At 4 miles, turn left on
Discovery Street then right at the **T**-in-
tersection to stay on Discovery Street.
Turn left on San Pablo Drive and begin
to wind your way through Lake San
Marcos Country Club. Turn left on La
Granada and start up a good invigorat-
ing hill. Turn right on La Plaza Drive
and glide along as it hugs the contours
of the Cerro de las Posas Mountains.
Avocado groves flank you on your left
and beautiful views of Lake San Marcos and surrounding areas fill your view
to the right. The road then begins a fast
descent toward the lake below. Once at
San Pablo Drive, turn left.

Cross over the bridge across Lake
San Marcos, then turn right on Lake San

Trip 8

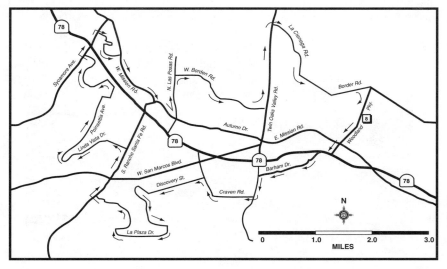

Marcos Drive and climb the short hill to the light at Rancho Santa Fe Road at 8 miles and turn right.

Cross San Marcos Boulevard and turn left at Linda Vista Drive. At the top of the short hill stay left on Linda Vista Drive. Turn right on Poinsettia Drive, then right on Oleander Avenue. Turn left on Smilax Road then left just before Highway 78 on Mimosa Avenue. Turn right on Oleander (currently Oleander is blocked from Poinsettia, but may connect in the near future.) Turn right again on Plumosa Avenue and follow the oleander-covered road as it meanders up and then down to Sycamore Avenue.

Turn right on Sycamore Avenue and cross under Highway 78. Turn right on Lobelia Drive then right again on Primrose Avenue. Primrose climbs slightly and circles its way around a hill with nice views of Vista to the west and north. Primrose turns into Plumosa (this section does not connect with the section you just rode south of Highway 78.) At Poinsettia, turn left and then right on Rancho Santa Fe Road.

Turn left on North Las Posas Road and follow it north through the new Santa Fe Hills development that is eating its way into the nearby hills. Turn right on Border Road and pass by Cerro de las Posas Park complete with a community swimming pool. Border Road climbs a bit then rewards you with a nice downhill run with views to the south and east.

Turn left at Twin Oaks Valley Road and follow it north by the Twin Oaks Golf Course. You can ride in the striped bike lane or in the San Marcos Trail system bike lane also on the right. Turn right at La Cienega Road and right again on Mulberry Drive. Mulberry angles past the San Marcos Cemetery on the left and becomes Rose Ranch Road. At Border Road, turn left then right on Woodland Parkway to return to Woodland Park.

Options: After passing through the Lake San Marcos area, turn left on Rancho Santa Fe Road. Then left again on Questhaven Road and right on Elfin Forest Road to add a beautiful ride along eucalyptus-shaded Escondido Creek. Turn left on Country Club Drive then left on Progress Place, right on Corporate Drive, then left on Meyers Avenue. At Barham turn left, then right on Woodland Parkway to return to the park. If you followed all these turns, this ride is 23 miles long.

San Marcos Loop

Trip 9. Discovery Creek Loop

Starting Point: San Marcos
GPS: Lat/Long 33° 6′ 56″, 117° 10′ 3″;
UTM 11S 484384mE 3663930mN
Distance: 2.5 miles
Elevation Gain: 50 feet
Riding Time: 30 minutes
Road Conditions: Smooth dirt trails,
smooth pavement
Traffic Conditions: Light
Difficulty: *
Equipment: Mountain bike

Nestled in the hills of San Marcos is a little known lake and creek that provides a quiet place to ride and enjoy the water habitat. The trails around Discovery Lake and along Discovery Creek are part of the San Marcos City Master Trails Plan that will eventually have 72 miles of interconnected trails. This easy, mostly flat ride takes you around the lake and along the creek and provides views of

the creek habitat and the Cerro de las Posas Mountains to the south. Except for several brief street crossings, the ride is free of auto traffic.

As in the Double Peak Climb, this ride begins at the parking area of Discovery Lake Park in San Marcos. Exit Highway 78 at Twin Oaks Valley Road; turn right on Craven Road, then left on Foxhall Drive.

From the parking lot there are several ways to start your loop around the lake. Pick any route ahead of you and follow the flat paved road around the lake. Chaparral covers the south end of the lake and a riparian habitat takes over below the dam. Many birds find this area to their liking, including herons, coots, and mallards. A slow pace is warranted

Trip 9

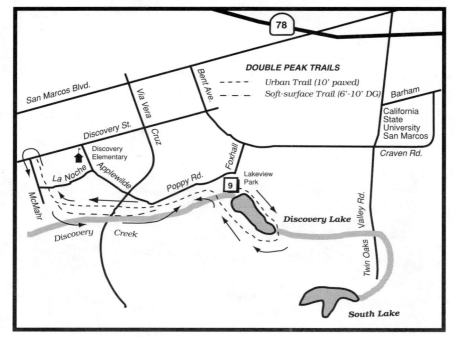

Discovery Creek Loop

through this area due to the hikers and rollerbladers that share the trail.

Back at the parking lot area, head west down a small hill. Shortly the trail splits; take the paved trail that parallels the north side of the creek. The trail crosses several streets as it follows the creek. The foliage along the creek provides shelter for many animals including quail, coyotes, and even deer and bobcats now and then. The trail ends at the school located at La Noche Drive and McMahr Road.

Follow the dirt trail on the south side of the creek to return to Discovery Lake.

Options: Just west of Applewilde Drive, the south trail splits. Follow the left split up a short, steep hill near Cima Drive. You can exit onto Cima Drive or continue as it becomes the Cima Trail. This route is moderately difficult and requires a mountain bike. This route is described in the options section of the Double Peak Climb trip.

Trip 10. Double Peak Climb

Starting Point: San Marcos
GPS: Lat/Long 33° 6' 56", 117° 10' 3";
UTM 11S 484384mE 3663930mN
Distance: 5 miles
Elevation Gain: 850 feet
Riding Time: 2.5 hours
Road Conditions: Graded and rough dirt roads, narrow single track in places, smooth pavement (for a short distance)
Traffic Conditions: Light
Difficulty: ****
Equipment: Mountain bikes required

San Marcos currently boasts 15 miles of multi-use trails within its city limits and the San Marcos City Master Trails Plan calls for a projected 72 miles of interconnected trails in the future. The goal of the trail system is to provide residents and visitors an alternative means of circulation as well as recreational activities. The trail system includes urban, multi-use paved, and soft surfaced trails.

This moderately difficult ride climbs 2.5 miles from Discovery Lake to Double Peak, the second highest peak (1644 feet) in the Cerro de las Posas Mountains. It is one of the more difficult of these soft surface trails. A rough fire road currently runs the length of the mountain ridge. In the future, a 200-acre regional park will be located on the Double Peak ridgeline, with picnic and group campsites, an equestrian area, museum and amphitheater.

The view from the peak is breathtaking; north to Mount Baldy in the San Gabriels, San Jacinto Peak and San Gorgonio Mountain in the San Bernardinos, and the Palomar Mountains; west to the ocean and coastal lagoons; east to the Cuyamacas; and southeast to the Harmony Grove and San Dieguito River Valley. The Harmony Grove fire swept through these hills in October 1996 and many burnt plant skeletons remain. The coastal sage scrub and chaparral habitats, however, are making a quick recovery. It is best to start this ride early to avoid midday heat.

The ride begins at the parking area of Discovery Lake Park in San Marcos. Exit Highway 78 at Twin Oaks Valley Road; turn right on Craven Road, then left on Foxhall Drive. For a warm up,

Trip 10

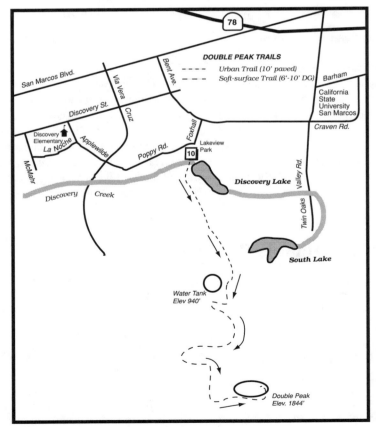

you may want to take a loop around the lake on the paved road.

To start the ride, cross the spillway bridge and the Discovery Lake Dam and head up the paved road just to the left of the water tank. Follow the rocky dirt trail at the end of the paved road to the left of the water tank labeled Double Peak Trail. You may have to walk in a few sections where it gets rocky. Where the trail divides above the water tank, take the left route. Watch for another Double Peak trail marker and turn right and continue on the trail until you reach the ridge above you. Don't forget to stop and look back down at Discovery Lake as it slowly recedes into the distance.

To climb Double Peak, turn left when you reach the dirt road on the ridge. In a short distance bear left and climb a small hill (the road to the right heads south and into the hills north of Questhaven). Follow the graded road as it climbs around the south side of the peak. Soon you will reach the top and the ruins of an old adobe brick house. You've earned a rest in the shade of an olive tree and hopefully cool ocean breezes from the west.

Options: To extend the ride 3 miles and an extra 400 feet of elevation and get a spectacular view directly down to San Marcos Lake, turn right when you reach the ridge instead of left. The rough road dips and climbs its way along the crest of the Cerro de las Posas Mountains. You will need to walk a particularly steep and rocky section about halfway to the microwave tower peak (1220 feet). A few hard to spot single tracks can be followed to bypass some of the steeper sections.

Another interesting approach to Double Peak is via the Cima Drive Loop. Instead of heading up the paved road by the dam, head west from the parking lot down a small hill. This trail soon splits and parallels both the north and south sides of Discovery Creek below the dam. Stay on the dirt trail that follows the south side as it passes by coast live oak and sycamore trees. The trail crosses Applewilde Street and through an area that was burned in the 1996 fire. At Cima Drive, follow the route that heads uphill. The trail follows a canyon and eventually reaches a saddle. At this point you can stay right to climb above the water tank and join the Double Peak Trail. Left will take you below the water tank to an old fire road. Right at the fire road takes you to the base of the Double Peak Trail and left drops you back to Discovery Lake.

Trip 11. Rancho Santa Fe

Starting Point: Rancho Santa Fe
GPS: Lat/Long 33° 1′ 12″, 117° 12′ 8″;
UTM 11S 481125mE 3653345mN
Distance: 4- or 11-mile loops
Elevation Gain: 300 feet (short loop); 800 feet (long loop)
Riding Time: 1.5 hours (both loops)
Road Conditions: Smooth roads with narrow shoulders
Traffic Conditions: Light to moderate
Difficulty: **
Equipment: Any multi-geared bike

A splash of color here, impossibly bright in the warm sunshine. A pungent coolness there, under the shade of the eucalyptus. Rows of citrus and avocado trees, marching in military precision over the soft hills. Horses and more horses, and white fences that seem to run for miles. Expansive homes that blend discreetly into their surroundings.

Welcome to Rancho Santa Fe, San Diego County's oldest and most mature planned community. Three million eucalyptus seedlings were planted here during the period 1906 to 1909 to provide wood for railroad ties, a project abandoned after it was discovered that eucalyptus wood was useless for that purpose. Many of these trees remain today, blanketing portions of "The Ranch" with a cool ambience of filtered sunshine. Homeowners have lavished attention on their outdoor landscaping, choosing carefully from the wide variety of exotic plants that do well in the local soils and climate.

People like to tour The Ranch in the fashion of Monterey's 17-Mile Drive—behind a windshield—but it's better to leave the car behind and explore by bicycle. Begin at the Spanish-styled business district, reached by way of Via de la Valle from Interstate 5. Try either or both of the loop trips outlined on our map, or simply improvise your own route. As a point of interest, in the 1930s the Francisco Building at the corner of Paseo Delicias and Via Santa Fe, currently occupied by Coldwell Banker, housed the only market and the first post office for Rancho Santa Fe. The building is now a California Historical Landmark.

The longer loop, 11 miles, takes you up and over several ridgetops, and swings around San Dieguito Reservoir,

Trip 11

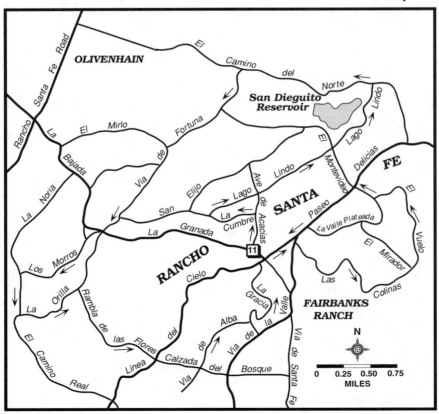

Rancho Santa Fe

and Calzada del Bosque in the vicinity of Linea del Cielo. Most of the route is well shaded.

On the shorter eastern loop, 4 miles over La Valle Plateada, El Vuelo and Las Colinas, you'll be out in the sunshine most of the time. The views extend to the east—miles of rolling hills backed by distant mountains, as far as the eye can see.

Options: The Fairbanks Ranch area, south of Rancho Santa Fe, offers more great sightseeing on a bicycle. One suggestion is a loop ride (not mapped here) following Via de Sante Fe, El Apajo, San Dieguito Road, El Camino Real, and Linea del Cielo. This 9.5-mile loop takes you past equestrian stables, thoroughbred farms, and the Fairbanks Ranch Country Club—site of the equestrian events staged during the 1984 Olympic games.

a storage facility for Colorado River water. The up and down grades aren't steep, except for Rambla de Las Flores

Trip 12. La Jolla Coast

Starting Point: La Jolla
GPS: Lat/Long 32° 50' 45", 117° 16' 9";
UTM 11S 474813mE 3634045mN
Distance: 7.5 miles
Elevation Gain: 320 feet
Riding Time: 1 hour
Road Conditions: City streets and bike path
Traffic Conditions: Light to moderate
Difficulty: *
Equipment: Any multi-geared bike

Twelve miles north and a world away from downtown San Diego, La Jolla basks in the natural air-conditioning of

the sea breeze. Although La Jolla technically lies within San Diego's city limits, the mostly affluent La Jollans regard their "village" as exclusive and distinct from the sun-baked suburbs sprawling for miles inland.

But La Jolla draws its share of tourists and office workers as well. Sometimes everyone seems to converge on this compact community at once, and traffic snarls are the result. To experience La Jolla's village flavor, you must cruise the back streets and the winding byways overlooking the ocean—as we suggest in this tour.

You may begin your ride on Park Row, south of Prospect Street and west of Torrey Pines Road, where curbside parking is usually abundant. Start by pedaling west on Prospect Street, but veer right on Coast Boulevard, dropping sharply down the textured pavement toward La Jolla Cove. From the concrete path overlooking the pocket beach at the cove, your eyes can usually trace the shoreline many miles north toward Oceanside.

Just south of the cove beach, the grassy expanse of Scripps Park lies open to the sun and sea air, bounded by a stately line of tall fan palms. You join Coast Boulevard, which continues past a curved breakwater—the Children's Pool

and the many seals that congregate here now—and meanders south, eventually returning to Prospect Street. From there, bike route signs direct you generally southward, with many turns, along the top of the low bluffs. If you miss seeing a sign, just remember to stay as close to the coastline as possible without turning down dead-end streets.

At Neptune Place, the route returns to the sand and surf. This is Windansea Beach, a surfers' favorite. Continue south on Camino de la Costa and Chelsea Avenue, then jog right to Calumet Avenue. Along the way you'll pass several of La Jolla's blufftop mansions and a number of mini-parks offering panoramic vistas of the ocean below.

Trips 12, 13

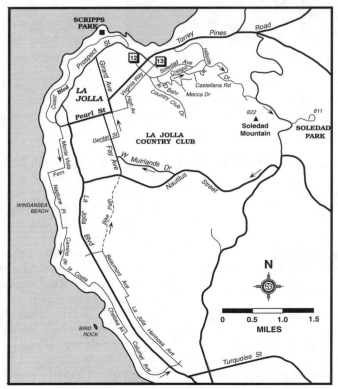

Calumet Avenue bends east, becomes Sea Ridge Drive, and intersects La Jolla Boulevard. Cross here and go one more block to La Jolla Hermosa Avenue. Ride north on this quiet street, again following bike route signs. You'll turn right (east) for one block, then north on Beaumont Avenue.

After a few blocks, Beaumont Avenue ends, but a narrow bike path continues ahead, traversing the base of a hill. The path crosses two small bridges, then stay right at a split in the path. The path climbs a hill and leads to the south end of Fay Avenue at Nautilus Street. Ride north on Fay Avenue, but skirt the congested main streets by going right at Genter Street, left on Girard Avenue, right on Pearl Street, left on High Avenue, and right on Virginia Way. Turn left on Ivanhoe Avenue and cross busy Torrey Pines Road at the traffic light. Afterward veer right and arrive at Park Row, your starting point.

Trip 13. Soledad Mountain

Starting Point: La Jolla
GPS: Lat/Long 32° 50′ 50″, 117° 16′ 0″; UTM 11S 475057mE 3634191mN
Distance: 5.8 miles
Elevation Gain: 800 feet
Riding Time: 1.5 hours
Road Conditions: City streets and bike lanes
Traffic Conditions: Light to moderate
Difficulty: ***
Equipment: Any multi-geared bike with low gears

For a unique look at La Jolla—from bottom to top—climaxed by the awe-inspiring view from the top of Soledad Mountain, try this short but challenging ride. As you pedal up the narrow byways overlooking La Jolla and the coast, you'll enjoy the same kind of visual amenities that many of La Jolla's residents live with everyday. You'll also encounter at least two very severe uphill grades that will require either "granny gears" or the patience to walk and push your bike.

Locate a parking space somewhere near the intersection of Torrey Pines Road and Prospect Street, and start from there. Go over to nearby Exchange Place and begin riding southeast (uphill). Soon Exchange Place splits into Country Club Drive on the right and Soledad Avenue on the left. Take the latter. After one block on Soledad, go right on Al Bahr Drive. Climb straight up the west flank of Soledad Mountain and follow a curious curlicue under and then over a gracefully curved, arched bridge. At the top of the curlicue, turn right on Crespo Street.

Homes in this part of La Jolla range from modest-looking cottages to elaborate villas, but all share the same million-dollar view of La Jolla Bay and the North County coastline. Some are perched precariously on stilts, anchored to solid ground on one side only.

After the hairpin turn on Crespo, look for the intersection of Mecca Drive on the right. An optional side trip up this dead-end street takes you a little higher to two stupendous overlooks.

Ahead on Crespo Street, look for the inconspicuous intersection of Castellana Road, where you veer right. Just ahead, you can visit a hidden overlook at the point where Puente Road, a stubby cul-de-sac, passes over Castellana Road on an arched bridge similar to the one seen earlier. From there, tall trees frame a view of tile rooftops and La Jolla Bay.

La Jolla Shores coastline from Mecca Drive

Next, back up a little and follow Castellana as it goes under the bridge and descends to meet Hillside Drive. Turn right on Hillside and follow its steep and winding course upward along the north slope of Soledad Mountain. Turn left on Rue Adriane and follow it to Via Capri, where you turn right. A very steep pitch lies ahead, after which you'll see the entrance of Soledad Park on the left.

From the Easter Cross steps, the metropolitan view is nearly complete, except toward the west where a part of Soledad Mountain's flat-topped summit intervenes. The newly emergent urban skyline of University City—now known as the Golden Triangle—lies directly below in the east, and the ever-changing skyline of downtown San Diego lies south. The park itself, though small, has grassy areas good for picnicking, and a water fountain that usually works.

After a well-deserved rest, return to the entrance and turn left on La Jolla

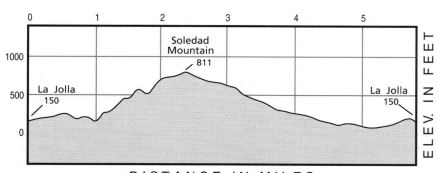

DISTANCE IN MILES

Scenic Drive. You soon reach Nautilus Street—the fastest way to complete the trip. Nautilus Street has a striped bike lane that is well away from the traffic lane and parked cars, making for a relatively safe, exhilarating downhill run. After about one mile, turn right on West Muirlands Drive. After another couple of minutes, turn right on Fay Avenue. Now thread your way—as in Trip 6— along the bike route behind La Jolla's

central business district to return to the starting point.

Options: Soledad Mountain Road and La Jolla Mesa Drive/La Jolla Scenic Drive are two other popular ways to reach Soledad Mountain by bicycle. Both provide convenient connections to Pacific Beach and Mission Bay to the south.

Trip 14. Around Mission Bay

Starting Point: East Mission Bay
GPS: Lat/Long 32° 47' 24", 117° 12' 31";
UTM 11S 480463mE 3627834mN
Distance: 12.5 miles
Elevation Gain: Almost flat
Riding Time: 1.5 hours
Road Conditions: Bike paths and city streets
Traffic Conditions: Moderate
Difficulty: *
Equipment: Any bicycle

San Diego's ever-popular Mission Bay Park includes 4200 acres of water and recreational land, and boasts an impressive 19 miles of sandy shoreline. Water-oriented sports are king here, but casual cycling is popular too because of the flat terrain and an extensive network of paths for strolling and bike riding.

This isn't a ride for speed demons. You'll be sharing parts of the route with runners, walkers, and roller skaters, some of whom seem to move in random, unpredictable ways. Allow plenty of time to gaze out over the sparkling waters of the bay and—like everyone else—get an eyeful of the sun worshippers.

A good place to begin is near the Visitor Information Center at the foot of Clairemont Drive on Mission Bay's east shoreline. Early in the day, it's easy to

secure a parking space in one of the many parking lots there.

Ride south along the meandering sidewalk at the bay's edge (or, if the sidewalk is impossibly clogged with foot traffic, you can use East Mission Bay Drive). After less than two miles you pass the entrance to Fiesta Island, an ungroomed expanse of sand dredged from the bottom of Mission Bay during the construction of Mission Bay Park in the 1950s. Five miles of lightly traveled road encircle this somewhat stark and unappealing island, offering good opportunities for high-speed bicycle workouts if you feel up to it.

Just before reaching busy Sea World Drive, turn right on a new paved biking and hiking path that heads west along the shore of Pacific Passage, the jet ski area south of Fiesta Island. Just before the path heads into the South Shores Boat Ramp stay left and then left again onto South Shores Park Drive. Cross over Sea World Drive at the light then turn right on the bike path along the north rim of the San Diego River flood channel and the Southern Wildlife Preserve. Looking down on the water (or mudflats if the tide is out) you may spot various shorebirds, including egrets, herons, terns and cormorants.

The bike path passes under two bridges, then connects with Quivira Way, south of Quivira Basin. Quivira Way continues west to a turnaround, where you can park your bike and begin a possibly interesting diversion by walking west on the jetty that divides the entrance of Mission Bay from the San Diego River channel.

Our route, however, curves around to Quivira Road, giving access to West Mission Bay Drive. Cross over the water via the wide bridge, then turn left at Mariners Way. There you can pick up another path following the perimeter of Mariners Basin. Soon you'll swing around Mission Point, near Mission Bay's narrow mouth. Continue west and arrive at the south end of Mission Beach, where you'll join the long Ocean Front Walk fronting the Pacific Ocean. This is San Diego's equivalent of Los Angeles' Venice Beach—the best place in town to show off, to see and be seen. The old, refurbished roller coaster and indoor swimming pool ahead are part of the resurrected Belmont Park. Nearby, along Ocean Front Walk and also

Trip 14

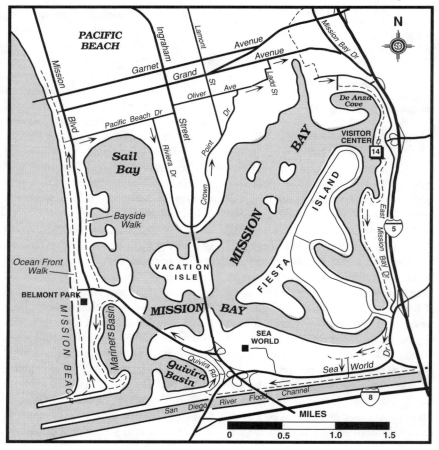

along Mission Boulevard (one block inland) are several good eateries offering the usual beachfront fare.

As an alternative to Ocean Front Walk, you could ride along the quieter Bayside Walk, which runs north of West Mission Bay Drive to a point just short of Pacific Beach Drive.

Six blocks short of the landmark Crystal Pier, you'll leave Ocean Front Walk as you turn right on Pacific Beach Drive. Follow it just a mile inland, and then turn right on Riviera Drive. Ahead, you'll round the nose of Crown Point, crossing over at the traffic light on Ingraham Street to reach Crown Point Drive. Ahead, you may glimpse a rather small area of natural marshland along the bay's north shore. Today it's a wildlife refuge, giving a glimpse of commonplace Mission Bay as it was in the days before dredging began.

Wend your way north and east through residential streets to Grand Avenue, where you turn right. Immediately after passing over the Rose Creek inlet, turn right on the narrow pathway that goes south and east (next to a ballfield) and joins East Mission Bay Drive at De Anza Cove. By either street or sidewalk, the starting point is now just a couple of minutes away.

Options: When you reach South Shores Park Drive, stay right and follow a bike path that hugs the southern end of the Sea World parking area. You eventually reach Perez Cove Way where you can turn right on Ingraham Street to head into Pacific Beach and follow Riviera Drive to Pacific Beach Drive then Mission Boulevard. Alternatively, at Perez Cove Way cross over Ingraham Street and follow Dana Landing Road to West Mission Bay Drive to continue across to Quivera and back to the starting point or right to follow the remainder of the ride above.

Trip 15. Point Loma Peninsula

Starting Point: Collier Park (near Ocean Beach)
GPS: Lat/Long 32° 44' 49", 117° 14' 5"; UTM 11S 478019mE 3623064mN
Distance: 16.5 miles
Elevation Gain: 1000 feet
Riding Time: 2 hours
Road Conditions: City streets and bike lanes
Traffic Conditions: Light to moderate
Difficulty: **
Equipment: Any multi-geared bike

The Point Loma peninsula, one of the most graceful and beautiful natural features of the San Diego area, offers many aspects. Its urbanized north end includes some of San Diego's most desirable residential districts. Its midsection hosts the U.S. Navy's Fort Rosecrans Reservation and other military facilities. Perched on the south end is the smallish Cabrillo National Monument, one of San Diego's most visited attractions. Just above the water's edge at the southern tip perches the Coast Guard Lighthouse, a familiar feature to mariners and San Diego residents alike. To see the best of this on two wheels, follow our somewhat devious (busy-street-avoiding) tour down and back up the peninsula.

Begin at Collier Park, a small neighborhood park one block north of Voltaire Street near Nimitz Boulevard. From there make your way—as suggested by the arrows on our map—southwest toward Sunset Cliffs Boulevard over the grid of residential streets overlooking Ocean Beach. As an alternative, you could loop through the more congested, but livelier sections of Ocean Beach closer to the surf.

Beyond Point Loma Avenue, Sunset Cliffs Boulevard takes you south along the brink of sculpted sandstone bluffs whose name aptly suggests their rosy tint at sundown. These wave-battered, structurally weak cliffs are receding at a rate that is among the fastest anywhere along the California coast. Elaborate retaining walls have been constructed to try to halt the advancing ocean.

At Ladera Street, turn inland and pedal up a steep two blocks to Cornish Drive. Go left and continue on Cornish past Hill Street to Novara Street. (Hill Street may be used to short-cut our route, but it is very steep.) Curve right, following Novara Street, then Santa Barbara Street. The climb takes you past immaculately kept homes, some with fabulous views of Mission Bay, Soledad Mountain, and the La Jolla coast. Use Tarento Drive, crossing Hill Street again, to reach Catalina Boulevard. Turn right and head south toward Cabrillo Monument.

Catalina becomes Cabrillo Memorial Drive as you enter the Navy reservation—the road is usually open to the public from 9 a.m. to 5 p.m. You can now ride in the comfort of a bike lane on the road shoulder. The final stretch of 2.5 miles runs right over the undulating spine of the peninsula. Take time to appreciate the extraordinary vistas of the Pacific Ocean and San Diego Bay, framed in places by myriad rows of military gravestones marching down the hillsides.

Just before you reach the big parking area for the monument, a road branches right toward the "new" Coast Guard lighthouse and tidepool areas. That's an interesting side trip, though the climb back up involves a lot of effort. Topside, you'll find the Visitor Center, a whale-watching overlook, and Point Loma's "old" (in use from 1855 to 1891) lighthouse—one of the eight original beacons along the California coast. A small fee is now being levied for all visitors to the monument.

From the old lighthouse you can sometimes spot San Clemente Island, 70 miles west, and the San Bernardino Mountains, 100 miles north. More commonly visible are Baja's Coronado Islands, some 20 miles to the south.

Retrace your path on Cabrillo Memorial Drive and Catalina Boulevard, but turn right onto Rosecroft Lane, 0.3 mile past the Navy reservation gate. Follow our arrowed route along Silvergate Avenue; Dupont Street; Gage Drive; Charles Street (this is a short, but very steep uphill); Bangor Place; and Golden Park Avenue. Pause at Lucinda Street and decide whether you want to ride or walk your bicycle down the vertiginous stretch of pavement ahead. The view—straight down to the San Diego Yacht Club harbor and across the bay to the downtown skyline—is classic.

At the bottom of the Lucinda Street hill, curve around to Armada Terrace and continue descending to Talbot Street. Jog left to Evergreen Street, then later Willow Street, passing modest but well-kept homes, many owned by local fishermen of Portuguese descent. You can avoid riding on busy Nimitz Boulevard, but you must cross it somewhere. This can be done at Capistrano Street—or at the traffic light on Chatsworth one block away.

Old Lighthouse

Pedal uphill on Capistrano to Tennyson Street, then go right and continue sharply uphill to Willow Street. Turn left on Willow and freewheel down through the stylish Loma Portal district. Unfortunately Loma Portal's amenities do not include peace and quiet, as it lies directly under the flight paths of aircraft departing from nearby Lindbergh Field.

The remainder of the route takes you down along residential streets on Loma Portal's west side, overlooking Mission Bay and Ocean Beach.

Options: If you want to abbreviate this trip, try using either Catalina Boulevard (north of Chatsworth Boulevard) or Santa Barbara Street to reach the southern half of the Point Loma peninsula from Collier Park.

Trips 15, 16

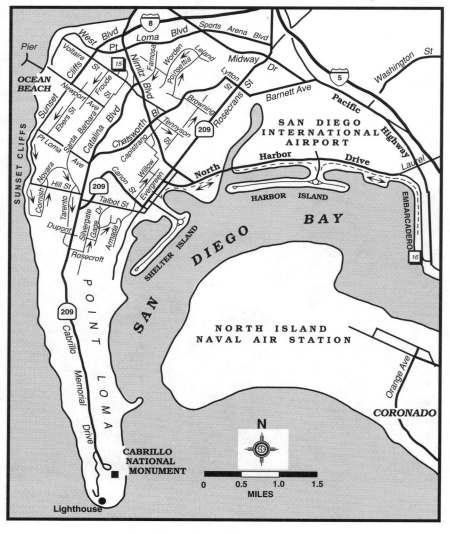

Trip 16. San Diego Bay Tour

Starting Point: Foot of Broadway, San Diego
GPS: Lat/Long 32° 42' 56", 117° 10' 20"; UTM 11S 483867mE 3619583mN
Distance: 16 miles
Elevation Gain: Almost flat
Riding Time: 1.5 hours
Road Conditions: Bike paths, sidewalks and city streets
Traffic Conditions: Moderate
Difficulty: *
Equipment: Any bicycle

If you really want to impress your out-of-town guests, invite them on this easy ride around Harbor and Shelter islands. Tourists and San Diegans alike flock to these man-made islands for fishing, picnicking, sunset strolls, and for a great view of downtown San Diego's gleaming skyline across the placid waters of the bay.

This bike ride is practically a land-based equivalent of the Harbor Cruise

"short tour" that departs from the pier at the foot of Broadway. You're seldom far from the water, and the ease of touring over virtually flat terrain lets you concentrate on the sights. Water and public restrooms are available at frequent intervals. Free parking within a short distance of the foot of Broadway is usually abundant if you arrive early on a Saturday or Sunday.

Start by wending your way north along the Embarcadero, passing the Maritime Museum's *Star of India* sailing ship and possibly a tuna boat that can still call San Diego home port. Beyond the stately County Administration Center, a durable concrete seawall has replaced the old wood-planked Embarcadero, flower beds, and paved paths that accommodate bicyclists and pedestrians. This is no place for speed, especially later in the day when walkers and runners jam the way.

Foot traffic thins as you follow the marked path (mostly a concrete sidewalk now) west along Harbor Drive toward the airport. Reaching the interchange for the airport and Harbor Island, you come to a marked pedestrian/bicycle crosswalk. Cross Harbor Island Drive there. The bike path continues north and west—but this is a good place to leave it and begin a side trip around Harbor Island. You can first explore the west end, then the east end.

The island—actually an artificial sandbar created by dredging operations in the bay—supports a mix of hotels and restaurants and a long, linear public park. You must stay on the island road, since the sidewalk next to the water is expressly reserved for pedestrians. To the south you'll spot the Navy's North Island

Embarcadero Bike Path

facility, where aircraft carriers frequently dock for maintenance. Harbor Island's east end is a good place to stop and admire the cityscape. This area is a favorite of photographers whose photos of the skyline appear in calendars and postcards.

Back at the island entrance, resume your travel west on the marked bike path. After about one mile, a bike-route sign directs you onto the Harbor Drive bridge, which goes over an arm of the bay. Continue west, passing some Navy facilities and two traffic lights, to a frontage road on the left. At the Sun Harbor Marina, turn left and then right on the sidewalk that curves left around the boat docks and sportfishing terminals (this can

be slow going when the tourists are out).

Work your way around to Scott Street, and then down Shelter Island Drive toward Shelter Island. This is Harbor Island's close cousin, with the same mix of private and public development. Here, too, you'll have to stay on the road, as bikes are prohibited on the scenic walkway. Still, there are opportunities to stop and picnic on the grass.

The trip back to the foot of Broadway can be a quick one if you want it to be. Use Scott Street to reach Harbor Drive, then retrace the marked bike path paralleling Harbor Drive. To make fast time, some riders like to stay on the eastbound shoulder of Harbor Drive.

Trip 17. Coronado

Starting Point: Ferry terminal, Coronado
GPS: Lat/Long 32° 41′ 52″, 117° 10′ 8″;
UTM 11S 484157mE 3617605mN
Distance: 5 miles
Elevation Gain: Almost flat
Riding Time: 30 minutes
Road Conditions: Wide residential streets
Traffic Conditions: Light to moderate
Difficulty: *
Equipment: Any bicycle

Separated from San Diego's dense urban core by no more than a mile of open water, the town of Coronado is an anachronistic, but engaging mishmash of old mansions, tidy bungalows, modern suburban houses and expensive new condominium complexes. Symbol and centerpiece of the town is, of course, the century-old, Victorian-style Hotel del Coronado. Somehow, Coronado has managed to retain a small-town atmosphere. It has become a kind of refuge for military retirees, including quite a number of admirals.

From a cyclist's point of view, getting around town could hardly be easier. Coronado's highest elevations are only about 30 feet. Broad, curving boulevards and quiet residential streets lace the town, inviting leisurely exploration.

To introduce yourself to the charms of Coronado, try following the short route mapped here—but do let yourself at any time be drawn down other avenues that may pique your interest. A good starting point is the ferry landing off First Street, two blocks east of Orange Avenue.

(There's no direct way to ride from "mainland" San Diego to Coronado, but cyclists now have the option of shuttling across the bay from downtown San Diego on the new and popular pedestrian/bicycle ferry—see Around the South Bay trip for more information.)

From the ferry terminal, pedal west on First Street past Orange Avenue, where, on the right, the old wooden Coronado Ferry ticket booth stands in the middle of a pocket park. Eighteen years passed between the demise of this

Downtown from Coronado

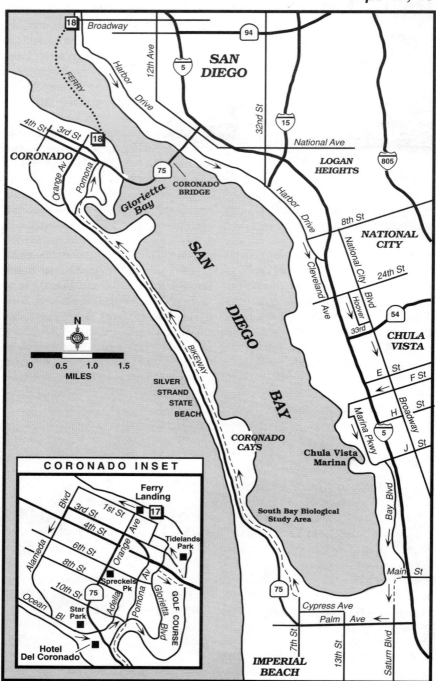

A bayside park in Coronado

star pines touch the sky, while bougainvillea, hibiscus and jasmine creep over the garden walls.

On the west side of Ocean Boulevard you will discover one of San Diego County's broadest and most beautiful beaches. The fat strip of sand here is partly the result of automobile-carrying ferry (after the Coronado Bridge was completed in 1969) and the inauguration of the new ferry service in 1987. Ride on, discovering two more tiny bayside parks on the right.

Each of these parks offers a superb view of the San Diego skyline that looms across the water. From the westernmost park, at the foot of I Avenue, you can often get a close-range view of one or two aircraft carriers docked at the North Island Navy maintenance facility.

A left turn on Alameda Boulevard sends you away from the bay and toward the Pacific Ocean shoreline. Alameda curves gently left and then slides into Coast Boulevard in the heart of a residential area of considerable historical and architectural interest. Styles range from Victorian and Tudor to Spanish mission. Several houses here were designed by noted early San Diego architects William S. Hebbard and Irving Gill. As elsewhere in the older nooks of Coronado, the mature subtropical landscaping delights the eye. Tall palms and dredging in San Diego Bay. Ocean currents have caused excess sand to pile up in a strip as much as 200 yards wide.

Ocean Boulevard curves left, becoming Dana Place at the Hotel del Coronado. When you reach the traffic light, cross Orange Avenue and continue curving left. Veer right onto Adella Avenue, then go right on 10th Street to join Glorietta Boulevard. Glorietta Boulevard weaves its way along the bay side of Coronado, separated from the water by the green links of the Coronado Municipal Golf Course. Stately homes line the other side of the street. Just before you reach 4th Street (the busy approach lanes to the Coronado bridge) turn right onto the signed bike path. The path skirts the golf course, passes under the bridge, and curves into the popular Tidelands Park. Ride out to the park entrance, and wend your way a few blocks north and west back to the starting point at the ferry landing.

Trip 18. Around the South Bay

Starting Point: Foot of Broadway, San Diego
GPS: Lat/Long 32° 42' 56", 117° 10' 20";
UTM 11S 483867mE 3619583mN
Distance: 24 miles
Elevation Gain: 100 feet
Riding Time: 2 hours
Road Conditions: City streets, bike lanes, and bike paths
Traffic Conditions: Moderate to heavy in a few places; no motorized traffic on bike paths
Difficulty: **
Equipment: Any multi-geared bike

It's a bit like driving on a lonely coastal highway, except that the "road" is an eight-foot-wide pathway, and your vehicle has just two skinny tires. The ocean lies on one side, the bay to the other. Gulls and terns wheel overhead on the sea breezes. Across the bay, the blue arc of the Coronado bridge frames the high-rise towers of downtown San Diego. Your tires whoosh softly over asphalt, and the broken white line slips steadily under the whirring machinery of sprocket and wheel.

After years of piecemeal construction, the Coronado-Imperial Beach bikeway is now complete. Following the route of an old railroad bed paralleling the Silver Strand highway, the bikeway is entirely separated from automobile traffic except where access roads cross. One way to explore it is by riding out and then back, starting from either Coronado or Imperial Beach—a round-trip distance of about 16 miles.

Another way (mapped here) is to begin in downtown San Diego, loop around the south arm of San Diego Bay, arrive in Coronado, and then return to your starting point via the San Diego Bay ferry. Currently the ferries are running every hour on the half-hour for the Coronado-to-San Diego direction (and every hour on the hour for the opposite direction). Call the San Diego Harbor Excursion, operator of the line, at 619-234-4111, to verify the schedule.

It bears repeating that you'll get the most out of this ride, and the other urban rides in this book, if you start early on a Sunday morning. Begin at or near the foot of Broadway (which is the east terminus of the ferry), and head south on Harbor Drive. Continue through the construction maze ahead, past Seaport Village, past the tall, new hotels and condominium towers that are reshaping the skyline, and past the mammoth San Diego Convention Center.

Using a marked bike lane on Harbor Drive's shoulder, continue riding southwest into San Diego's shipbuilding district. On your right is National Steel and Shipbuilding. Later, the big Navy base at the foot of 32nd Street comes into

view. (*Safety reminder:* Watch for railroad tracks cutting obliquely across the pavement during the next few miles. Cross these at right angles if possible, or dismount if necessary.)

When Harbor Drive turns east to join Interstate 5, bear right on Cleveland Avenue in order to stay parallel to but west of I-5. After 0.6 mile, turn left on 24th Street, and cross under I-5 and over the San Diego Trolley tracks. A bit farther ahead, turn right on Hoover Avenue. Hoover curves left to become 33rd Street. Next, make a right turn at the first opportunity. This puts you on National City Boulevard, which crosses the South Bay Freeway (Highway 54) and the Sweetwater River flood channel, and soon becomes Broadway.

Continue on Broadway about one mile to F Street. Turn right and pass over I-5, heading for the bay shore. Soon, you go left (south) on Marina Parkway. After a couple of jogs right and left, you'll

be skirting Chula Vista's Marina View Park and its small-boat harbor. You then end up on J Street, heading back inland toward Chula Vista. Make a right on Bay Boulevard just before you reach I-5.

Among the sights now in view on the right are a big, oil-fired power plant and Western Salt's evaporation ponds and processing plant. Notice the huge pile of salt.

Beyond the salt works, Bay Boulevard bends left and joins a frontage road along the west side of I-5. Continue south to Main Street, where you can pick up a short segment of bike path connecting to Saturn Boulevard. Upon reaching Palm Avenue (a major thoroughfare) turn right and go 0.8 mile west to 13th Street. Go right on 13th, left on Cypress Avenue and right on 7th Street, passing through a residential area.

At the north end of 7th Street, you can pick up the delightful bikeway leading to Coronado. Diversions along the way include the South Bay Biological Study Area, with its abundant bird life, and Silver Strand State Beach. The state beach includes visitor facilities on both sides of the Silver Strand—the quiet bay side and the breezy, cooler Pacific side.

When you approach the "Hotel Del," you can either stay on the bikeway to join Glorietta Boulevard and follow the last part of the route we describe in the Coronado trip above; or you can follow Orange Avenue (or streets parallel to it) through Coronado's center. In the latter case, it's easiest to cross busy 3rd and 4th streets at Orange Avenue, where there are traffic signals.

Aim for First Street, just east of Orange Avenue, where you'll find the ferry terminal. After boarding, the ferry will whisk you and your bicycle across the bay in less than ten minutes.

Trip 19. Bonita - National City - Skyline Tour

Starting Point: Skyline
GPS: Lat/Long 32° 41' 50", 117° 1' 3";
UTM 11S 498351mE 3617541mN
Distance: 13 miles
Elevation Gain: 600 feet
Riding Time: 2 hours
Road Conditions: City streets
Traffic Conditions: Moderate
Difficulty: **
Equipment: Any multi-geared bike

The Sweetwater River is a pleasant place to cruise along on your bike, enjoying the riparian habitat and sloweddown pace. We will follow the river for a short distance on its journey through Bonita then swing north through National City and east into Skyline.

To find the starting point, take the South Bay Parkway to Worthington Street and park near the corner of Worthington Street and Paradise Valley Road. Start pedaling south on Worthington Street. Follow it across the South Bay

Parkway as it changes its name to Sweetwater Road and starts plunging downhill.

The Sweetwater County Park on your left is owned and managed by the County Department of Parks and Recreation. The site includes approximately 60 acres of riparian habitat along the Sweetwater River. Just upstream is the Sweetwater Dam, a major engineering feat and San Diego County's first major dam completed in the late 1800s that supplies water for National City and Chula Vista. If you have the time, there are benches overlooking a small lake where you can watch waterfowl and gaze on San Miguel and Mother Miguel Mountains to the east.

Soon you will pass by the Bonita Golf Club on your left and Rohr Park.

Trip 19

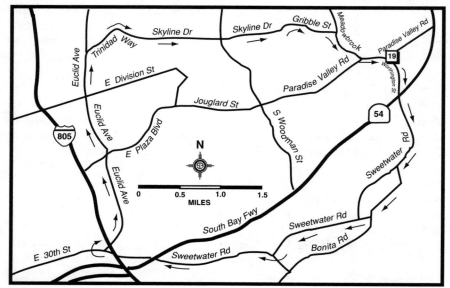

At 3.5 miles stay right on Sweetwater Road at the junction of Willow Street. From here you leave the Sweetwater River area and begin a slow climb to a crest and then downhill past the Plaza Bonita shopping center that opened in 1983.

Cross under Interstate 805 and make an immediate right on Euclid Avenue. Follow Euclid Avenue as it gently rolls north through National City. Turn right on Trinidad Way not far after Logan Avenue. Stay left as you pass Santa Maria. Continue east as Trinidad Way becomes Skyline Drive.

Skyline Drive, with its wide lanes and striped bike lanes, starts climbing through southern Encanto and Skyline. Soon you pass the Martin Luther King Jr. Memorial Park and municipal pool on the right. Turn right on Meadowbrook Drive then left on Paradise Valley Road to return to your starting point.

Options: From Sweetwater Road take Bonita Road across the Sweetwater River and follow it west along the opposite of the river following the Sweetwater Open Space Preserve. At either Willow Street or Plaza Bonita Road cross back over the Sweetwater River to continue the ride as described above.

Trip 20. Balboa Park

Starting Point: Balboa Park
GPS: Lat/Long 32° 43′ 53″, 117° 9′ 30″; UTM 11S 485158mE 3621330mN
Distance: 10.3 miles
Elevation Gain: 700 feet
Riding Time: 1.5 hours
Road Conditions: City streets and bike paths
Traffic Conditions: Light to moderate
Difficulty: **
Equipment: Any multi-geared bike

Balboa Park, 1400 lushly landscaped acres smack dab in the middle of San Diego, is a true centerpiece of recreational, cultural and educational opportunity. The park boasts a dozen major museums, sports facilities, meeting rooms, the world-famous zoo, and a good portion of relatively untouched open space. Set aside as public land in 1868, the park gained many of its picturesque buildings during the Panama-California Exposition in 1915-16 and the California-Pacific Exposition in 1935-36.

This tour visits nearly all of Balboa Park's famous attractions, and will introduce you to some of its lesser-known back corners. Sunday mornings

Trip 20

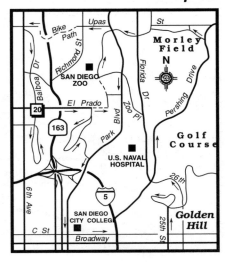

are best, when car traffic is minimal. As in most big-city parks in recent years, crime and homeless people are no strangers to Balboa Park. Even though cyclists are seldom the target of threatening behavior, it is probably wiser to ride in groups rather than alone while exploring here.

Begin at Laurel Street near Sixth Avenue on the park's west side. Head south on gently curving Balboa Drive, which soon becomes a one-way loop. At the south end, you can pause at a scenic overlook featuring a view of the downtown high-rises to the south.

After returning to Laurel Street, turn right, heading east. The roadway, now called El Prado, spans a deep canyon via the tall, arched Cabrillo Bridge. Today traffic on the 163 freeway roars through the canyon, but during the 1915-16 exposition a quiet "lagoon" occupied the canyon floor below.

The cluster of Spanish-Colonial buildings on the far side of the bridge includes the landmark, 200-foot-high California Tower. The Old Globe theater, Alcazar Gardens, and a half-dozen museums lie a few minutes away—all best explored by securing your bike and proceeding on foot. Another worthwhile diversion on wheels takes you south from El Prado past the Organ Pavilion to another cluster of buildings, most dating from the more recent exposition of 1935-36.

Back on El Prado, continue east on a stretch of roadway closed to auto traffic. Just short of the fountain, turn left on Village Place. Village Place bends east—but you keep going north on a pathway toward the zoo entrance. Continue, bounded by the zoo fence on the left and the huge zoo parking lot on the

right. When you reach Park Boulevard, turn right, heading south.

On Park, you can coast downhill over Interstate 5 and down to C Street, where there's an obligatory left turn opposite the San Diego Trolley tracks. Follow C Street east, up a steep hill, to 25th Street. Turn left on 25th and ride north into the Golden Hill section of Balboa Park. A paved loop there offers unique vistas of the downtown skyline, Point Loma, San Diego Bay and a bit of the Pacific Ocean.

After rounding the loop road, go east a short block to the oddly named 26th Street Road, which will take you downhill to Pershing Drive. Then go uphill—steep at first—on Pershing. San Diego's Municipal Golf Course lies on the right as you climb, while mostly vacant land—once a landfill—is on the left. Farther to the left (west) you'll see see the mammoth Naval Hospital on the slopes of Florida Canyon.

Near the top of the long grade on Pershing Drive, bear left on Jacaranda Place. Then wend your way west through the parking area in front of the Morley Field sports complex. Morley Field features tennis courts, a municipal pool, and a velodrome (bicycle track).

Continue west on Morley Field Drive—down a steep hill to Florida Drive and then up a steep grade to Park Boulevard. Jog right on Park to Upas Street, where you make a left turn. Continue on Upas to its end, where a paved path takes you across the 163 freeway on a narrow, ivy-covered bridge. On the far side of the bridge, veer right on the concrete path and ride (or walk your bike) up to the flat, grassy area above. There you can pick up eucalyptus-shaded Balboa Drive, and return south to your starting point.

Trip 21. Mission Hills - Banker's Hill

Starting Point: Presidio Park
GPS: Lat/Long 32° 45′ 26″, 117° 11′ 34″;
UTM 11S 481943mE 3624193mN
Distance: 6.5 miles
Elevation Gain: 300 feet
Riding Time: 1 hour
Road Conditions: City streets and
suspension footbridge
Traffic Conditions: Light to moderate
Difficulty: *
Equipment: Any multi-geared bike

Two of San Diego's most distinctive and interesting old neighborhoods are explored on this tour. Within a block or two of the route outlined here lie more than a dozen homes and buildings cited in San Diego's historical register. Although you can rush through in less than one hour, it's better to allow plenty of time and follow our suggestions for exploratory side trips.

Begin at Presidio Park, southeast of the I-5/I-8 junction, just above Old Town State Historic Park. From the upper end of the park, above the Serra Museum, follow Presidio Drive up the hill and into Mission Hills. This is one of San Diego's oldest and most classy places to live, with beautifully landscaped streets and stately, well-crafted Spanish-style homes.

Turn left at Arista Street, then right on Fort Stockton Drive. After about half a mile, bear left onto Lewis Street, following the designated bike route. The tiny, refurbished business district on Lewis Street has the look of prosperity once again. North of here you can explore at your leisure the network of "not a through" and "no outlet" streets overlooking Mission Valley.

At Goldfinch Street, turn right and pedal south to Washington Street in the heart of Mission Hills' shopping area.

Turn left on Washington, then right at First Street, heading south again. Streets crossing First Avenue soon begin to assume names in reverse alphabetical order— Upas, Thorn, Spruce, etc. (The sequence of tree names continues south to Cedar, Beech, and Ash streets in downtown San Diego.)

A right turn at Spruce Street puts you in the core of the Banker's Hill district, so named for the many prominent citizens who once lived there. The work of the early twentieth-century architect Irving Gill, recognized today as one of the trendsetters in modern building design, is well represented here. So too is the work of his partner, William Hebbard, and several of Gill's proteges including Richard Requa and Frank Mead. Within a four-block radius of First and Spruce are many examples of their handiwork and influence.

Continue west on Spruce Street to discover the remarkable suspension footbridge that spans one of the deep canyons hereabouts. Built in 1912 to give access to streetcars that ran along Fourth Avenue, it has recently undergone extensive repair. Walk, don't ride, your bike across the swaying bridge—70 feet above the canyon floor—and admire the eucalyptus and pepper trees, palms, and carpets of wild grass below.

On the far side of the bridge, continue west on Spruce Street and turn left on Curlew Street. (If there's time, you might try exploring the many stately homes in the blocks to the north, afterward returning to Spruce and Curlew.) From Curlew, bend right on Palm Street, and then go left on Dove Street. Stay right at the next bend, and follow Eagle Street down to Reynard Way. Turn right and head north (uphill) on Reynard Way, a wide thoroughfare following a canyon bottom. Reynard becomes Goldfinch Street, which continues north into Mission Hills.

A slight variation of our earlier route now takes us left (west) on Fort Stockton Drive, then left on the delightful, palm-lined Sunset Boulevard. When Sunset begins to curve right, make a sharp right on Witherby Street. Then circle the head of a canyon by going left on Hickory Street and left on Trias Street. After a final right turn on Presidio Drive, you'll arrive momentarily at Presidio Park.

Trip 21

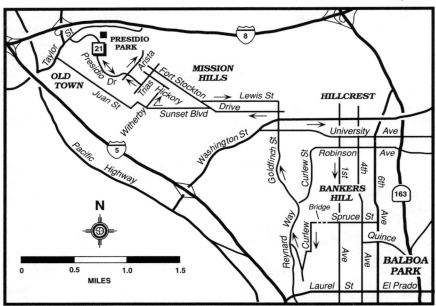

Trip 22. Kensington

Starting Point: Kensington (East San Diego)
GPS: Lat/Long 32° 45' 46", 117° 6' 22"; UTM 11S 490071mE 3624815mN
Distance: 6 miles
Elevation Gain: Almost flat
Riding Time: 30 minutes
Road Conditions: City streets—some bumpy
Traffic Conditions: Light
Difficulty: *
Equipment: Any bicycle

Kensington is probably the most interesting of San Diego's distinctive neighborhoods to tour on a bicycle. The effort is almost trivial—you simply glide along, admiring the well-kept homes and landscaping. The best feature, though, is an almost complete lack of traffic. Most of Kensington was built prior to World War II on a mesa overlooking Mission Valley. Although it is now almost completely surrounded by freeways in the canyons below, the streets themselves consist mostly of long, looping drives and numerous cul-de-sacs. Kensington was one of the first neighborhoods to break out of the rectilinear mold.

Kensington's developer bestowed English place names on the streets, yet the houses here are typically Spanish-style with red tile roofs. Behind the rows of palms, every lawn seems meticulously trimmed, flowers grow in profusion, and nearly every home offers a bright, freshly painted face to passing onlookers.

You may start at the small park and library on Adams Avenue between Kensington Drive and Marlborough Avenue. Go south on Marlborough, and follow the circuitous counterclockwise route shown on our map. It's easy and carefree to follow since nearly all the turns are to the right. Exploring the several dead-ends is optional, but don't miss the east extension of Ridgeway, where many of the finest homes in the area can be found.

Options: The neighborhoods of Normal Heights, west of Kensington, and Talmadge, east of Kensington, feature the same kind of quiet, curving streets. Normal Heights can be reached by way of Adams Avenue; Talmadge can be reached by way of Aldine Drive.

Trip 22

Trip 23. Lake Miramar

Starting Point: Lake Miramar (near Mira Mesa)
GPS: Lat/Long 32° 54′ 45″, 117° 6′ 7″; UTM 11S 490475mE 3641398mN
Distance: 5.0 miles
Elevation Gain: Almost flat
Riding Time: 30 minutes
Road Conditions: Narrow paved road
Traffic Conditions: Light
Difficulty: *
Equipment: Any bicycle

The five-mile perimeter road around Lake Miramar is a real magnet for the exercise minded. On any given Sunday morning, hundreds of self-propelled travelers are busy making the circuit around the 5-mile perimeter road. Others picnic, fish, or take to the water in

small boats. Swimming and wading are not allowed since the water in the lake is stored for domestic use.

The reservoir itself, perched halfway up the dry hills overlooking Mira Mesa and the coastal plain, was completed in 1960 as part of the Second San Diego Aqueduct project. Water shipped south into the lake originates from both the Colorado River Aqueduct and the California Aqueduct. In a year of average rainfall these two sources satisfy more than 90 percent of San Diego County's water needs. An important component in the City of San Diego's emergency water storage system, Lake Miramar is kept nearly full all the time.

Lake Miramar

Not long ago, San Diego's creeping suburbia was out of sight from most parts of the lake, but today condominiums and tile-roofed houses soar like battlements on some of the surrounding hillsides. Still, there's a sense of splendid quiet and peacefulness as you breeze along the convoluted perimeter road, taking in the wild scents of sage and chaparral.

The road is virtually flat throughout and carries only a small amount of traffic—mostly fishermen and picnickers who drive around the east end of the lake

to the fishing piers and picnic area on the north side. A one-mile stretch of the road, including the passage over the dam, is free of auto traffic. *Note:* The road across the dam may be closed for security reasons.

The earthen Miramar dam stands 150 feet above the reservoir bottom. To the west the drop is precipitous toward I-15 and the sprawl of Mira Mesa. The often hazy view stretches over a carpet-like expanse of eucalyptus trees in nearby Scripps Ranch, and extends to Miramar

Trip 23

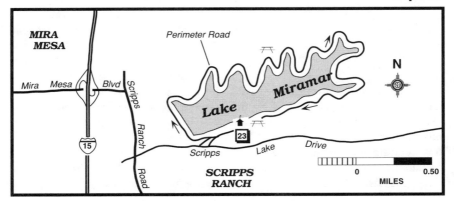

Naval Air Station and Kearny Mesa. In somewhat clearer weather Soledad Mountain and the emerging "Golden Triangle" skyline punctuates the horizon to the west. Ocean views can be had from here during clear-weather episodes in late fall and winter.

Since there's little shade along Lake Miramar's shore, it's often best to ride in the morning or early evening, or on cool, overcast days. In springtime, much of the native vegetation on the hills above is in bloom, creating a feast for both the eyes and the nose.

Trip 24. Tierrasanta Duo

Starting Point: Tierrasanta
GPS: Lat/Long 32° 50′ 2″, 117° 6′ 4″; UTM 11S 490540mE 3632688mN
Distance: Road ride: 6 miles, Trail ride: 4 miles
Elevation Gain: 800 feet
Riding Time: 1 hour road, 1.5 hours trail
Road Conditions: Smooth, paved roads with narrow to wide shoulders or easy dirt trails
Traffic Conditions: Moderate
Difficulty: **
Equipment: Any multi-geared bike for the road section. A mountain bike for the trails

Tierrasanta, Spanish for "Holy Land," was part of Camp Elliot during World War II, a sprawling 13,000-acre artillery and tank training range. Tierrasanta is nestled in the hills and mesas between Interstate 15, Admiral Baker Golf Course, and Mission Trails Regional

Park and is described by some locals as "The Island in the Hills."

Clean-up work has continued over the years to remove unexploded shells from old Camp Elliot. Some may still resurface due to erosion, so you will notice signs throughout the area warning you not to touch any such items. In 1983 two 8-year-olds were killed while playing with a live explosive they found in the hills. But our off-road route should be safe as we stay on relatively smooth, well-used dirt trails.

This ride has two parts: a short road bike route that covers only 6 miles but gives you a good flavor of Tierrasanta with great views of Mission Trails and Cowles Mountain to the east. And if you have a mountain bike, additional multi-use trails follow the canyon bottoms that provide a very different picture of the more rural canyon atmosphere of Tierrasanta.

Road Ride

To reach the starting point, head east on Tierrasanta Boulevard then north on Santo Road. Park on one of the cul-de-sacs west on Antigua Boulevard. Head north on Santo Road and turn right on Portobelo Drive. The road climbs as you pass by Shepard Canyon to your right. Portobelo Drive turns into Via Vallarta.

Turn left on Clairemont Mesa Boulevard and follow it to the end to see the Tierrasanta entrance to the 5,700-acre Mission Trails Regional Park. If you're on a mountain bike you can explore many trails in the area.

Head west on Clairemont Mesa Boulevard and turn left on Rueda Drive and then left again on Calle de Vida. You will pass by another entrance to Mission Trails and then skirt the edge for a short distance with great views to the east of Mission Trails and Cowles Mountain. The road changes to Colina Dorada Drive and begins a great downhill run. Keep an eye out for Admiral Baker Golf Course in the valley to your left.

Turn right at Tierrasanta Boulevard and begin regaining some of the elevation you just lost. Once at Santo Road, turn right and cruise down to Antigua Boulevard where you parked your car. Optionally, you can turn left on Santo Road and follow it to the end and back to add a few extra miles to the ride.

Trail Ride

If you have a mountain bike, there are several multi-use trails through the canyons between the rows of houses that make for a great loop ride. Start this ride on any of the cul de sacs off of Antigua Boulevard west of Santo Road or at the small park where Amaro Drive meets Antigua. Tortuga Court, Bravo Court, Guincho Court, Matador Court, Carioca Court, or Veracruz Court are all cul-de-sacs and have paved trails at their ends feeding down into Shepard Canyon and a 337-meter multi-purpose trail. Head down any one of these trails and when the paved trail ends, turn left onto a good dirt trail heading east. (A small single track can be taken west here but ends pretty quickly at Clairemont Mesa Boulevard.)

Once you reach Santo Road, turn left and follow the sidewalk a short distance to Antigua Boulevard. Cross the street here and jog slightly right and past a gate to continue down the multi-use dirt trail eastward, paralleling Antigua. This is Greenbelt Park, a 2092-meter trail. The trail on the north side of the creek bed is for bikes and hikers, and the trail on the south side of the canyon is for hikers and joggers.

The canyon is filled with eucalyptus trees, scrub oaks, and other stream side vegetation and an occasional bench to rest and enjoy the quiet. Soon you will reach a small dam with a picnic bench and a small lake. Continue past the left side of the dam and at the **Y** in the trail stay right.

As you near the end of the canyon, the trail splits into three trails that climb rather steeply up to meet Via Vallarta. Continue to stay right to take the easiest and slightly longer way up. Once on Via Vallarta, turn left and keep an eye out for a trail that picks up on the right side of the road just past Via Playa de Cortes.

Follow the trail between the rows of houses as it slowly drops into a small canyon with the houses left high above you. You almost forget that neighborhoods surround you as you make your way along the trail here amongst the trees.

Near the end of the trail you may begin to hear the traffic on Highway 52 just north of here. The dirt road to your right climbs moderately then quite

Tierrasanta

steeply, ending up near Caminito Playa Catalina. From there you can drop down into a canyon and climb up the other side and into the western reaches of Mission Trails Park. This ride will continue to the left however. The next left will take you up a small trail that comes out on Portobelo Drive next to the Belsera condominium complex at Playa Baja (see Options for an interesting side trip).

Turn right on Portobelo Drive and blast down the hill. Just past the first speed bump look for the dirt trail that heads south and down into the canyon on your left. The trail will cross a dry creek bed and then climb up to meet Via Rica Way. Cross over Via Rica and down again to continue on the trail.

This section of trail passes through a eucalyptus forest paved with leaves.

After a nice ride, you will come out on Antigua Boulevard, just east of Santo Road where you entered the creekside trail not long ago. Head across Santo Road to end up back at the cul-de-sac in Tierrasanta where you started.

Options: If you are up for an adventure, instead of taking the left that exits at Portobelo Drive, continue straight up a small gravelly hill and take a small single track to the right across a small wooden bridge. This trail skirts the fence below Highway 52, passing a small lake, and eventually climbing up to Fortuna Mountain and into Mission Trails Park.

Trip 24

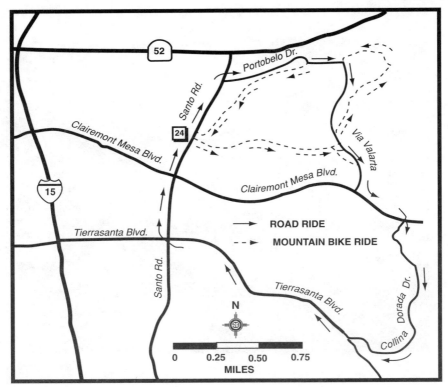

Trip 25. Lake Murray

Starting Point: La Mesa
GPS: Lat/Long 32° 47' 47", 117° 2' 11";
UTM 11S 496589mE 3628530mN
Distance: 6 miles (round trip)
Elevation Gain: Almost flat
Riding Time: 45 minutes
Road Conditions: Narrow, paved road
Traffic Conditions: Bicycle and foot
traffic only
Difficulty: *
Equipment: Any bicycle

Lake Murray is part of a new and important recreational resource—the 5700-acre Mission Trails Regional Park. The park, which includes the undeveloped open spaces of Cowles and Fortuna mountains along with portions of the San Diego River in Mission Gorge, is recognized as one of the largest urban parks in the United States.

The lakeshore parking lot is open seven days a week, from sunrise to sunset. You can also leave your car outside any of three entrances (Kiowa Drive, Murray Park Drive, and Baltimore Drive), wheel your bike through the pedestrian gates, and tick off as many miles as you desire along the paved perimeter road.

The perimeter road, which begins near the lake's main entrance on Kiowa Drive (off Lake Murray Boulevard, half a mile north of Interstate 8), extends for 3 motor-traffic-free miles around the east, north, and west shores. After swinging around five major and minor arms of the lake, the pavement comes to an end along the west shore, where NO TRESPASSING signs and a big fence discourage further exploration. It's not possible to loop completely around the lake—but you can simply return the way you came.

Because of the heavy foot- and skate-traffic on the road—weekdays included—this is not the best place to crank out some fast miles. But if you're looking for a relaxing spin at dusk with a cool breeze blowing off the lake, a more pleasant locale could scarcely be imagined.

Trip 25

Trip 26. Mount Helix

Starting Point: Eucalyptus Park (La Mesa)
GPS: Lat/Long 32° 45' 35", 117° 0' 1";
UTM 11S 499970mE 3624454mN
Distance: 6.5 miles
Elevation Gain: 1040 feet
Riding Time: 1 hour
Road Conditions: Narrow, winding
residential streets
Traffic Conditions: Moderate to heavy
on Bancroft and Fuerte; otherwise light
Difficulty: **
Equipment: Any multi-geared bike with
low gears

Few bikers tackle the slopes of
Mount Helix, the shaggy, conical promontory rising 1373 feet above sea level
in San Diego's eastern suburbs. The inclines are not easy, but the reward at the
top is a fabulous view stretching from
the Laguna Mountains on the east horizon to Baja's Coronado Islands offshore.
The foreground scenery is spectacular
too. Whether or not you aspire to own
such real estate, you can at least admire
and enjoy the fine architecture and landscaping as you ride by.

A good place to begin is Eucalyptus
County Park, located on Bancroft Drive
just east of the 125 freeway and about
one mile north of the 94 freeway. From
the park, pedal north on Bancroft about
half a mile to Fletcher Drive, and turn
right. After 0.2 mile, turn left on Mar-
guerita Lane that will take you to Lemon Avenue. Turn right there and continue
on a steeper grade to the stop sign at Alto
Drive. Turn right again and follow Alto
for another 1.1 miles of twists and turns
up the west and north flanks of Mount
Helix. The "crux" of this climb is a nearly
straight stretch—just before a hairpin
turn—with an incline of about 15 percent.

After the hairpin turn, the road climbs
only a little more and then contours along
Helix's north slope. Make a right turn at
Mount Helix Drive, following the sign
to the summit. Mount Helix Drive (one-
way for cars and bikes) carves a helical
path that loops up and then down the
mountain.

From the road crest, next to a tiny
parking lot, a short, steep pathway leads

Mount Helix Amphitheater

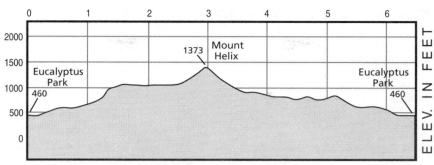

to the big white Easter cross on the mountain top. The amphitheater hewn from stone just east of the cross is used for Easter sunrise services and other special events. A drinking fountain near the lower level of the amphitheater usually dispenses cool water when it's most needed.

The trip back to Eucalyptus Park is, of course, fast. Descend Mount Helix Drive and Helix Drive toward Fuerte, but be ready to turn right on Vivera Drive after crossing a narrow bridge. At the foot of Vivera Drive, turn right on Fuerte Drive and follow it 0.4 mile south to Grandview Drive (this short stretch is uncomfortably narrow with fast traffic). Bear right on Grandview and proceed mostly downhill 1.5 miles to MacRonald Drive. Turn left and pedal over to Tropico Drive, which will take you back to Bancroft Drive near Eucalyptus Park.

Options: The narrow, winding residential avenues of Mount Helix are only a foretaste of the many interesting routes you can try in the rolling hills both north and south of there—an area roughly bounded by the communities of El Cajon on the north, La Mesa on the west, and Spring Valley on the south. A city street map will suggest many possibilities.

Trip 26

Trip 27. Fallbrook - De Luz Loop

Starting Point: Fallbrook
GPS: Lat/Long 33° 23′ 5″, 117° 15′ 5″;
UTM 11S 476622 mE 3693762 mN
Distance: 26 miles
Elevation Gain: 3520 feet
Riding Time: 3.5 hours
Road Conditions: Smooth roads with little or no shoulder
Traffic Conditions: Light
Difficulty: ****
Equipment: Any multi-geared bike

Much of the coastal mountain region of northern San Diego County and southwestern Riverside County has, until recently, been forgotten territory. Twenty years ago, the brushy hills and wooded backcountry canyons between Fallbrook and Temecula were sparsely inhabited—a few ranchers residing in rustic and sometimes tumbledown old houses. Today, agribusiness and estate housing is taking over, with palatial homes dotting the avocado and citrus groves. New roads are cut on the hillsides every year, while older dirt roads are being upgraded by paving. Still, traffic in the area remains light, and many of the oak-shaded canyons remain pristine.

This is anything but a flat tour. Whenever the pavement levels out, there's always some vicious uphill stretch just around the corner. Low gears are helpful, of course. Brakes must be in excellent operating condition. There are no stores along the way and water may not be easy to obtain, so plan accordingly.

Fallbrook's town center is a convenient and safe place to park your car and begin the ride—take Mission Road west from Interstate 15 or Mission Road north from State Highway 76 to get there. We assume you'll start from the corner of Mission and De Luz roads.

Pedal north on De Luz Road past some apartment buildings, and then coast down a twisting section of road through a shady ravine. The Santa Margarita River lies at the bottom of the grade, hidden at this point by a dense screen of riparian (streamside) vegetation. Sycamore, cottonwood, and especially willow trees are the hallmarks of this type of vegetation, which covers only one half of one percent of San Diego County's land surface. The Santa Margarita is considered to be the last major undammed watercourse in coastal southern California and supports some of the county's richest riparian habitat.

Upon reaching the river, veer left, staying on De Luz Road. After a mile you cross a wooden bridge over the river and begin an unyielding, 1.5-mile climb to the top of a divide. Gliding down the other side, you dip into the first of the many small, shady ravines you'll cross or follow in the next few miles. In a few spots, the live oak trees arch overhead to form a cool canopy, penetrated only by slender shafts of sunlight. On the open hillsides, the view stretches

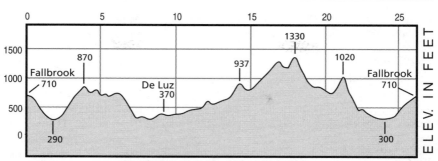

Trip 27

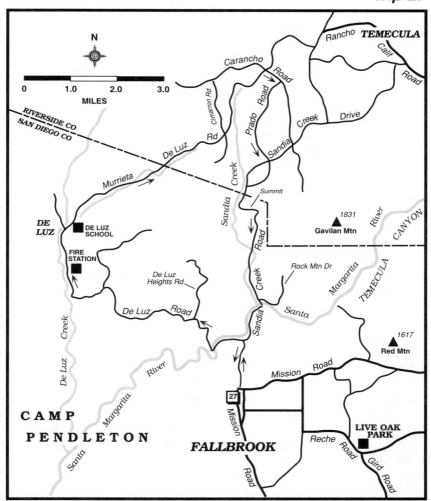

south and west to the rugged mountains of Camp Pendleton's interior. Look for hawks soaring on the thermals overhead.

After about seven miles (from Fallbrook) the road makes a decided curve to the north and follows the east bank of De Luz Creek, a tributary of the Santa Margarita River. After another mile you pass the De Luz Fire Station, where water is usually available during the warmer months. A tiny cluster of houses about 0.7 mile beyond this marks De Luz proper. While De Luz is possibly the county's smallest community today, sufficient population in the late 1800s warranted the establishment of a post office here.

At the road fork just beyond De Luz, bear right on De Luz-Murrieta Road. The old De Luz schoolhouse on the right, now an ecology center operated by the Fallbrook school district, has a nice front lawn perfect for lounging or picnicking. The brooding Santa Margarita Mountains form a backdrop to the west, rising to elevations of over 3000 feet.

De Luz-Murrieta Road rises steadily, following a tributary of De Luz Creek. Other than a short, steep climb up and over a hillside where the road shortcuts a meander in the creek, you'll be down close to the shady bottom of the creek for most of the next four miles. There are several creek crossings, mostly concrete dips. If water is present steer straight and don't pedal as you cross these dips—otherwise you risk a case of "road rash."

Ahead, the road curves right and climbs abruptly to pass over a saddle (intersection of Cimarron Road). Down the other side you join the bottom of Sandia Creek, another south-flowing tributary of the Santa Margarita River. Again, there is a delightful promenade of oak trees—and more fords. Presently the

road bends sharply right and ascends steeply for 0.6 mile to the intersection of Carancho Road. Turn right there, go 0.4 mile, and turn right on El Prado Road. Continue for about 0.7 mile to a summit affording a good view of the surrounding area. This is avocado country—part of the Rancho California development centered on the town of Temecula in Riverside County. Pumps and automatic drip-irrigation systems hiss in the groves.

There is a lot of downhill riding ahead. At the bottom of the grade you'll come to Sandia Creek Drive. Turn right and continue mostly downhill for about 1.5 miles. Sandia Creek is approached again, but only briefly. Instead of an expected gradual downhill run to the Santa Margarita River, the road turns sharply uphill to climb yet another ridge. For a while you're on a privately maintained segment of the road. A gut-busting, 300-foot climb is followed by a hair-raising descent—beginning with a 400-foot drop at about 20 percent grade. Take this slowly and cautiously!

You come alongside Sandia Creek again, and the smooth pavement resumes. At the next major intersection, stay right, cross the Santa Margarita River, and then follow the river toward De Luz Road and the one-mile climb back to Fallbrook.

Options: For a longer loop trip, remain on De Luz-Murrieta Road and continue to Rancho California Road. This will take you down to Temecula, where you can cross Interstate 15 and pick up Pala Road or Rainbow Canyon Road (see the Rainbow-Pala trip). You may complete this loop by going west on Highway 76, then north on Gird and Reche roads to central Fallbrook.

The many rural roads south and east of Fallbrook make fine cycling routes when traffic is light (especially Sunday mornings). Live Oak Park (corner of Gird and Reche roads) is a pleasant stop for a picnic.

Trip 28. Twin Oaks Valley Loop

Starting Point: Escondido
GPS: Lat/Long 33° 10′ 2″, 117° 5′ 26″; UTM 11S 491560mE 3669650mN
Distance: 12 miles
Elevation Gain: 500 feet
Riding Time: 1.5 hours
Road Conditions: Smooth paved roads with narrow to wide shoulders
Traffic Conditions: Light to moderate
Difficulty: **
Equipment: Any multi-geared bike

Sprawling suburbia is slowly taking over the northern reaches of Escondido and San Marcos but there are still a few nice places to ride. In springtime, a carpet of green spreads over the farmland of Twin Oaks Valley and the surrounding hills, suggesting what much of coastal California looked like in the rather recent past.

A good place to start this easy-going loop is Jesmond Dene Park in north Escondido. To get there by car, turn north from the east terminus of the Route 78 Freeway onto Broadway and continue 2.5 miles to the park entrance. Begin riding by turning south on North Broadway. After a couple of minutes, turn right onto Country Club Lane. It soon becomes a divided road with a landscaped median. Cross Centre City Parkway, pass under Interstate 15, and continue past the Escondido Country Club golf course.

After Country Club Lane reverts to an undivided road, pay attention: you must swing left (south) to stay on it. When you reach El Norte Parkway, turn right. Continue west on El Norte Parkway, which becomes Borden Road at the Bougher Road intersection. Continue another mile to Richland Road and the Richland Elementary School. Turn right on Richland Road, ride alongside the school grounds, and start a gradual climb. At the top of the rise ahead, pause to enjoy the view north and west into Twin Oaks Valley. Not surprisingly, the valley and settlement below was named after a pair of giant oak trees.

A curving, half-mile descent takes you down into the valley itself. Turn right on Mulberry Drive, left on Olive Street, and right on Sycamore Drive. After passing Walnut Grove Park, you bend left, staying on Sycamore, and cross a creek. Just ahead you reach moderately busy Deer Springs Road. Turn right and begin a 300-foot, 2.3-mile-long climb across a little range of hills called the Merriam Mountains. Interstate 15 lies on the far side.

Cross over the freeway and turn right on I-15's east frontage road, signed NORTH CENTRE CITY PARKWAY. Immediately ahead, just past a driving range, turn left on Jesmond Dene Road. It will take you three miles back to your starting point. These last relaxing, downhill miles are a fitting conclusion for the ride. Live oak trees arch overhead, dappling the pavement with shadows. During the wet months, a small creek trickles alongside the road as well, its melodious trill complementing the soft swishing of your tires and the quiet whirr of the chain and sprockets.

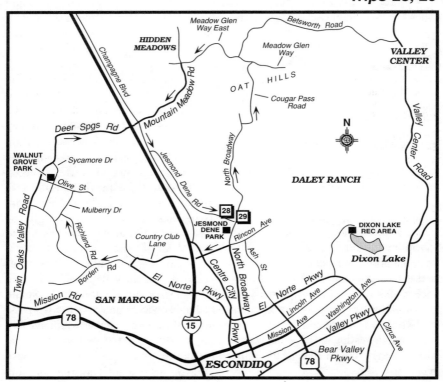

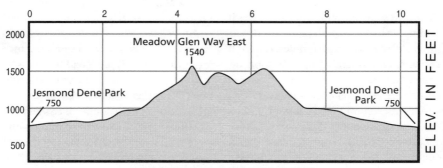

Trip 29. Cougar Pass - Jesmond Dene Loop

Starting Point: Escondido
GPS: Lat/Long 33° 10′ 2″, 117° 5′ 26″;
UTM 11S 491560mE 3669650mN
Distance: 10.5 miles
Elevation Gain: 1100 feet
Riding Time: 2 hours
Road Conditions: Paved roads with narrow to wide shoulders; graded dirt roads.
Traffic Conditions: Light
Difficulty: ***
Equipment: Mountain bike

Escondido's North Broadway loses no time as it slices from outlying housing tracts toward the wild, chaparral-covered hills north of town. North Broadway is your ticket to the intriguing, unpaved Cougar Pass Road, which will lead you to a summit with a great view of the surrounding countryside and the flatlands of Escondido.

To reach the starting point, turn north from the east terminus of the 78 Freeway onto Broadway and continue north 2.5 miles to Jesmond Dene Park. Park there, and start riding north on what is now North Broadway. Ahead, North Broadway slips into what is known as Reidy Canyon, named after Maurice Reidy who settled here in 1850. Reidy and his family moved to these foothills after searching for gold in northern California.

After about two miles, turn right onto the unpaved Cougar Pass Road (North Broadway dead-ends ahead). As you ascend, you'll pass a cactus farm on the left, a fitting reminder of the warm and dry climate of inland North County. In about one mile, you'll come to an area dotted with oak groves. One such grove near the roadside may entice you to stop for a spell and cool down in the shade. The area hereabouts was named the Oat Hills, after the wild oats that once grew

here. You will soon pass the western entrance to Daley Ranch on your right. Robert Daley became the first European to settle in the valley east of here, building a log cabin and later laying claim to the property in 1875. A number of ranch buildings still remain. Daley Ranch is now a 3,058-acre conservation area that offers over 20 miles of multipurpose trails for hiking, mountain biking, and equestrian use.

Ahead, several short stretches of the road have been paved. More pavement in out-of-the-way places like this can be expected in the future as Escondido's suburban sprawl expands toward the surrounding hills.

When you reach the top of Cougar Pass Road (after a particularly demanding uphill stretch), take some time to admire the view. On clear days, Escondido shimmers behind you, while rocky hills stretch to the north. Unseen below you, water is flowing south in the First San Diego Aqueduct. Here it passes through the 0.7-mile-long Oat Hills Tunnel.

Make no turns and you'll find yourself on Meadow Glen Way East, a paved road that will lead you back down toward civilization. You'll enter the secluded Hidden Meadows residential area, and wind along the Meadow Lake Country Club. The area boasts some whimsical street names: Cerveza ("Beer") Drive and Cerveza Baja ("Lower Beer").

Turn left on Mountain Meadow Road. You'll cut through the golf course, climb a bit, and then swoop down to Interstate 15, losing 550 feet of elevation in about three minutes. Turn left on North Centre City Parkway and continue parallel to I-15 a short distance. Just

past the driving range, turn left on Jesmond Dene Road. The area ahead, Jesmond Dene, is said to be named after
part of Newcastle-on-Tyne in England.
Enjoy the cool, downhill run on oak-
shaded Jesmond Dene Road. In a few
minutes you'll arrive at your starting
point.

Options: For a longer loop trip (20
miles), turn right at the Cougar Pass
Road summit and continue north (on

dirt) to Betsworth Road, where pavement
resumes. Follow Betsworth east to Lilac Road. Turn right there and right again
on Valley Center Road to reach the community of Valley Center, where a stop
may be in order for cold liquid refreshment. Continue south down the long
grade into Escondido and then turn right
on Washington Avenue. A right on Citrus, right on Ash, left on Rincon, and a
final right on North Broadway will take
you back to Jesmond Dene Park.

Trip 30. West Lilac Loop

Starting Point: San Luis Rey Downs
GPS: Lat/Long 33° 17′ 24″, 117° 12′ 56″;
UTM 11S 479923mE 3683274mN
Distance: 17 miles
Elevation Gain: 1280 feet
Riding Time: 2 hours
Road Conditions: Smooth roads with
narrow to wide shoulders
Traffic Conditions: Light
Difficulty: ***
Equipment: Any multi-geared bike

This rather short, but hilly route takes
you through some of rural North County's quintessential citrus/avocado and
horse ranching country. The highlight is
the crossing of the West Lilac Road

bridge, a striking, arched overpass over
Interstate 15. The bridge has become a
symbol of entry into San Diego County
from the north.

San Luis Rey Downs, consisting of
a rural subdivision and a golf course, is
a convenient place to begin. It is just east
of Highway 76 at Bonsall, about 12 miles
from Oceanside.

From the east side of the golf course,
pedal east on Camino del Rey, which
follows a broad valley. Old maps call this
valley Moosa Canyon. Today it is sparsely occupied by spacious country estates,
where many a racehorse is stabled.

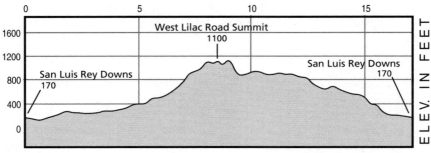

DISTANCE IN MILES

West Lilac Bridge

After about four miles, the flat, easy riding ends as Camino del Rey crosses under Interstate 15 and comes up to Old Highway 395. Turn right and pedal on a moderate uphill grade, still following Moosa Canyon's drainage. On the right you'll spy a resort and a small lake in the canyon bottom. After 0.9 mile, don't miss your turn to the left—Circle R Drive.

You now go uphill, skirting some new homes and a golf course on the valley floor below. You then start climbing the scrubby slopes to the north. After some twists in the road and much heavy breathing, you arrive on a rolling table-land dotted with small ranches. Just beyond the top of a particularly steep pitch ahead, Circle R Drive turns abruptly left (north) and intersects with West Lilac Road. Keep straight, taking the branch that leads west back toward San Luis Rey Downs.

In the next mile, you reach the last significant summit. From then on, the ride amounts to an almost effortless, breezy spin through rolling landscapes dotted with avocado and citrus orchards. When you reach the high bridge over Interstate 15, take time to stop and examine its structure. Down through the expansion joints at either abutment, you can spot the heavy cables that help support the hollow bridge.

In the final miles of descent—west of Old Highway 395—keep an eye out for the Pacific Ocean in the distance. In a few minutes, you'll be on flat land next to the San Luis Rey River, close to your starting point.

Trips 30, 31, 32, 33

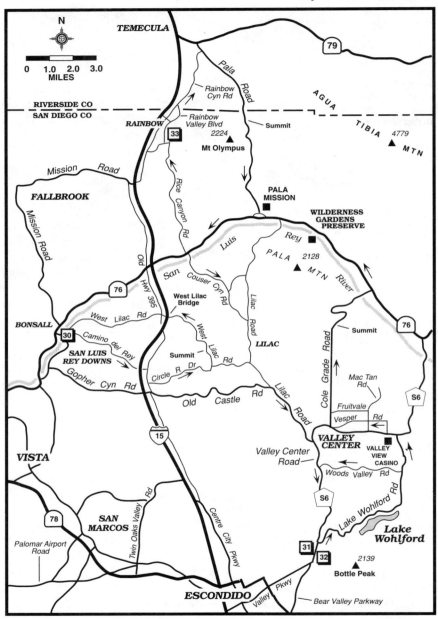

Trip 31. Valley Center Tour

Starting Point: Escondido
GPS: Lat/Long 33° 8′ 54″, 117° 1′ 59″;
UTM 11S 496921mE 3667543mN
Distance: 15 miles
Elevation Gain: 1250 feet
Riding Time: 2 hours
Road Conditions: Smooth, paved roads with mostly narrow shoulders
Traffic Conditions: Light to moderate, except moderately heavy on Valley Center Road and possibly Lake Wohlford Road due to the Valley View Casino
Difficulty: ***
Equipment: Any multi-geared bike

Resting high above the inland city of Escondido, Valley Center has become both a kind of rural suburb and a genuine agricultural producer. Citrus and avocado orchards spread across its hillsides. Oak-dotted pastures and grasslands cover the flatter terrain, broken here and there by new residences on spacious lots. Valley Center remains a great place to tour on a bike.

This ride, on the southern fringes of Valley Center, will give you ample opportunity to practice climbing skills as well as enjoy the beauty of a hidden reservoir—Lake Wohlford. On the oak-shaded country roads thereabouts, you'll feel as if you're a long way from the bustle of traffic in nearby Escondido.

A good place to start is on Valley Parkway at Las Brisas Drive (a minor residential street) on the northeastern edge of Escondido. This intersection is about 0.3 mile north of Bear Valley Parkway and 0.1 mile south of Washington Avenue. Ample curbside parking is available.

Cycle north on Valley Parkway for about 0.8 mile, and then turn right on Lake Wohlford Road. Immediately, you begin a 750-foot climb, hopefully assisted by the usual prevailing breezes, but possibly hindered by the absence of a cooling headwind. The road is rather steep and winding and has narrow shoulders. Near mile marker 2, the road begins to flatten after you cross a bridge over Escondido Creek. Very shortly you catch your first glimpse of the lake. Now the long climb is over.

The road ahead hugs the north shore of Lake Wohlford, passing a picnic area and a small store/resort. The next 2.2 miles consist of some easy riding through rolling hills of chaparral and oak. Near the upper (east) end of the lake, the road curves north, passes through pasture land, and skirts San Pasqual Indian Reservation lands. On the right you

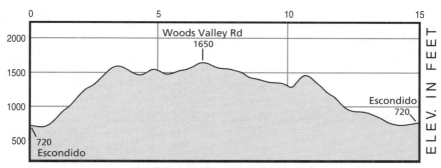

may hear the sound of water rushing through the Escondido Canal. It shunts water southward from the San Luis Rey River to feed Lake Wohlford, which belongs to a separate watershed.

At mile 6.7, just as you enter the scenic Woods Valley, turn left onto Woods Valley Road. This beautiful rural road carries you generally downhill through more pasture, wild grassland, and shade-giving oaks. Palomar Mountain is in view on your right. Steep-sided Bear Ridge lies to the left. You'll pass some citrus trees, and pumpkins in the fall. Don't miss Bates Nut Farm on the right, where every kind of nut and nut-related

confection may be bought and consumed.

At mile 10.7, Woods Valley Road ends at busy Valley Center Road. Valley Center's "center" with a few stores, lies a short distance to the right—but you turn left to complete the loop. After a 0.7-mile climb, you roll over a summit and start a fast, freewheeling, 3-mile descent. In the flatlands below, keep straight ahead at the Lake Wohlford Road junction. Continue past some roadside fruit stands—worth a stop for still more snacks—and return to the starting point.

Trip 32. Escondido - Pauma Valley Loop

Starting Point: Escondido
GPS: Lat/Long 33° 8′ 54″, 117° 1′ 59″; UTM 11S 496921mE 3667543mN
Distance: 47.5 miles
Elevation Gain: 4070 feet
Riding Time: 5 hours
Road Conditions: Smooth roads and highways with mostly narrow or no shoulders
Traffic Conditions: Light to moderate; moderately heavy on Valley Center Road and Lake Wohlford Road due to the Valley View casino
Difficulty: ****
Equipment: Any multi-geared bike

We've routed this tour along some of North County's most scenic, yet little-known rural roads. Valleys filled with citrus orchards and hillsides draped with avocado groves seem to be everywhere, along with remnants of the original vegetation—chaparral, oaks, and grasses. As is characteristic of the foothills of North County, this tour has its share of sweaty climbs and fast, refreshing downhills. On

warm days you'll probably want two water bottles for stretches of 15 or more miles without water. The Valley View Casino on Lake Wohlford Road now brings more traffic to this area, so an early morning start is advised.

We'll assume you're starting on Valley Parkway at Las Brisas Drive, and beginning this ride exactly as in the Valley Center Tour ride above. After passing Lake Wohlford and Woods Valley Road, you will pass by the San Pasqual Indian Valley View Casino on the left. Watch traffic through this area. In about 8 miles, turn left at the **T**-Intersection with Valley Center Road and continue west only 0.3 mile. Turn right on Sunset Road to escape the traffic. Then go left on Vesper Road, right on Mac Tan Road, and left on Fruitvale Road. This way will take you through some pleasant orange groves and over several small summits offering great vistas of Valley Center's

Cole Grade Road

agreeably rolling and bucolic terrain.

As Fruitvale Road ends, turn right on Cole Grade Road. After several ups and downs, the road dips precipitously. For a moment you seem airborne as the orchard-carpeted Pauma Valley suddenly comes into view nearly a thousand feet below. The valley floor slants up sharply to meet the base of the Palomar Mountains in the distance, creating an almost aerial perspective.

With wide, banked turns and an average grade of 9 percent, Cole Grade is arguably the most exciting downhill stretch of pavement in San Diego County. It is also very easy to pick up too much speed here, and the winds can be unpredictable. So keep both hands on the brake levers!

At the bottom, you ford the San Luis Rey River on a usually-dry concrete ford. A one-mile climb from there brings you to Highway 76. Turn left on the highway and pedal westward down the valley of the San Luis Rey.

After passing the entrance to Wilderness Gardens Preserve County Park, the road climbs a bit, offering a fine view of the cottonwood- and oak-shaded river bottom. Next stop is Pala, with its picturesque mission (see the Rainbow-Pala trip). Don't forget to top off your water bottles there.

Four miles beyond Pala, you turn left on Couser Canyon Road, an obscure gem of a back road. Cross the San Luis Rey River on a rustic wooden bridge and continue south across the valley and up onto the slopes above. After some twists and turns, you sidle up to the trickling creek, which is draped in a glorious canopy of oaks and wild grapevines.

The road now climbs more briskly, attaining a 1170-foot summit. It then drops sharply to join Lilac Road—stay

right. Up ahead, after 0.8 mile, the road dips to cross Keys Creek in the shade of huge oaks. Don't blink, or you'll miss the tiny community of Lilac, named after the ceanothus, or California lilac, that once grew in abundance here.

After three more miles, Old Castle Road intersects on the right. Make a left turn to stay on Lilac Road, and complete the rather uneventful remaining distance to Valley Center's bustling center. Turn

Lilac Road

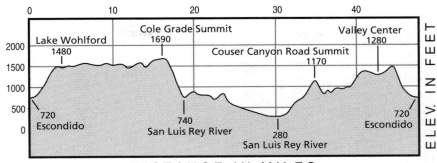

right on busy Valley Center Road, go up and over a small pass, then relax as you coast downhill to the flat stretch just short of the starting point.

Options: You can divide this trip into two shorter loops by using Valley Center Road as a connector. The northern loop (Cole Grade Road/Couser Canyon Road/Lilac Road) is the more scenic of the two. You can also try combining the northern loop with the Rainbow-Pala Loop.

Trip 33. Rainbow - Pala Loop

Starting Point: Rainbow
GPS: Lat/Long 33° 24′ 37″, 117° 8′ 48″;
UTM 11S 486352mE 3696582mN
Distance: 23 miles
Elevation Gain: 1350 feet
Riding Time: 2.5 hours
Road Conditions: Smooth roads with narrow or no shoulders
Traffic Conditions: Light; moderate on Highway 76
Difficulty: ***
Equipment: Any multi-geared bike

Like our Fallbrook-De Luz Loop tour, this one, too, passes through Riverside County for a while, looping through the outskirts of Temecula. Highlights include a visit to the serene Pala Mission, and a delightful, curving downhill run on Pala Road.

To reach Rainbow, a good starting point, exit Interstate 15 at Mission Road, then follow Old Highway 395 north to Rainbow Valley Boulevard. Turn right, and go east about a mile to an intersection where Rainbow Valley Boulevard turns sharply north. Find a parking spot nearby and begin cycling north through the verdant valley blessed with the name "Rainbow." Curiously, the place name has nothing to do with the optical phenomenon; rather it refers to Mr. J.P.M. Rainbow, who helped lay out the townsite in 1888. Two years later, Rainbow was elected a San Diego County Supervisor.

After about 1.5 miles, Rainbow Valley Boulevard joins Old Highway 395. Continue north over a road summit and begin a twisting descent to the flat floor of Temecula Valley. Beyond the valley, you can often spot the 10,000-foot-plus summits of San Jacinto Peak and San

Pala Mission

Gorgonio Mountain, 35 and 50 miles away respectively.

Beyond the golf course at the bottom of the hill, turn right (southeast) on Pala Road and begin a long, gradual climb back into the foothills. For a couple of miles, housing developments crowd the landscape, but soon you're back in the country again. After an elevation gain of about 250 feet, a sign announces the San Diego County line.

Once over the gentle summit ahead, you begin the exhilarating spin toward Pala. The wild-looking slopes of the canyon, clothed with a mature growth of chaparral, frame a view of range after range of blue-tinted mountains. The downgrade ends abruptly, and a final, nearly flat mile takes you right into the Indian settlement of Pala.

On the left you'll pass Pala Mission, founded in 1816 as an *asistencia* (submission) of Mission San Luis Rey, and still in use today. Stop to admire the carefully restored chapel, the pleasant gardens, and the original bells in a free-standing campanile.

A somewhat unexciting three miles follows as you go westbound on busy Highway 76 through the valley of the San Luis Rey River. Then a right turn on Rice Canyon Road takes you away from traffic again. This paved country lane meanders uphill, gaining about 700 feet, and then drops into a ravine packed with a dense growth of live-oak trees. After an additional few hundred yards, the road bends right, leaving the canyon, and climbs another 200 feet to reach a corner of Rainbow Valley. Turn left at the **T**-intersection and you'll soon come to your starting point.

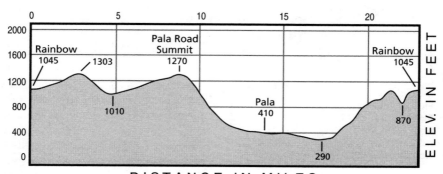

Rice Canyon Road

Trip 34. Harmony Grove - Questhaven Tour

Starting Point: Escondido
GPS: Lat/Long 33° 6′ 30″, 117° 6′ 31″;
UTM 11S 489866mE 3663124mN
Distance: 16 miles
Elevation Gain: 830 feet
Riding Time: 1.5 hours
Road Conditions: Smooth roads with narrow shoulders; 1 mile of dirt road
Traffic Conditions: Light to moderate
Difficulty: **
Equipment: Any multi-geared bike

Harmony Grove, Questhaven and Elfin Forest roads, just minutes away by car or bicycle from Escondido's center, offer the kind of rural serenity once common in North County, but now confined to just a few special places. For years, Escondido residents called this area "Spook Canyon" because of the spiritualists who once held meetings here.

Begin at the corner of Hale Avenue and Harmony Grove Road, where curbside parking is abundant. Hale Avenue may be reached by 9th Avenue or Valley Parkway from Interstate 15. The suburban edges of Escondido recede quickly as you round several corners on Harmony Grove Road and begin a series of gentle curves along the eucalyptus-shaded bank of Escondido Creek. On weekdays, huge trucks may pass you at first, but this traffic disappears beyond the quarry area about 1.5 miles from the starting point. After passing Country Club Drive, the road enters the live-oak-shaded San Elijo Canyon, where the hillsides pinch in tightly and the creek below tumbles over polished boulders. You'll have a better view of the creek on the return leg of the trip.

Five miles from the start you'll come to what remains of the old Elfin Forest Resort on the left. At this point, turn right on obscure Questhaven Road—leading up through a tangle of live oaks. After a short distance the pavement turns into a graded dirt road. A small brook trickling beside the road delights the ear, while the great, luminescent masses of poison oak delight the eye.

When the road rises onto the sunny slopes, look for blooming Cleveland sage, monkeyflower, Mariposa-lily, and a dozen other wildflowers. The blooming of native vegetation continues well into June. After one mile (near the Questhaven Christian Retreat), pavement resumes but the climb continues. Beyond an area of fine rural homes, a large patch of chaparral covers the hillsides to the left. A more poetic term for this type of vegetation is "the elfin forest," hence the local place name.

The road crests, dips, then climbs again. Beyond the second summit the road thankfully starts downhill. Unfortunately, the tentacles of suburbia are reaching this area too quickly. The area to the north and west is under construction for a housing development and a shopping area. The road makes a bend right to skirt construction and now runs close to the hills to your right. After a nice downhill and a four way stop, continue through the new development. Don't miss the left turn at Elfin Forest

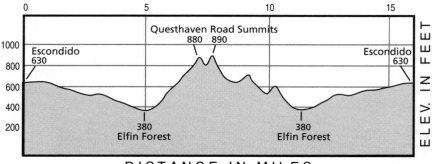

Questhaven Road

Road. Elfin Forest Road is somewhat less scenic, but mostly downhill for awhile. Water is available at the volunteer fire department or at the Elfin Forest stage stop on your left as you drop down towards the old Elfin Forest Resort. On the final leg of the trip back to the starting point, however, you can enjoy once again the pleasant ride through San Elijo Canyon.

Options: The Questhaven/Elfin Forest road loop can be approached from Rancho Santa Fe Road near La Costa, as well as from Escondido.

A longer loop incorporating Elfin Forest or Questhaven roads can be made by taking Rancho Santa Fe Road south to El Camino del Norte, El Camino del Norte east to Del Dios Highway, and Del Dios Highway east and north back to Escondido. Turn left on Avenida Del Diablo, then right on Hale Avenue to return to your starting point. Del Dios Highway is heavily traveled, but it has bike lanes along most of its shoulder.

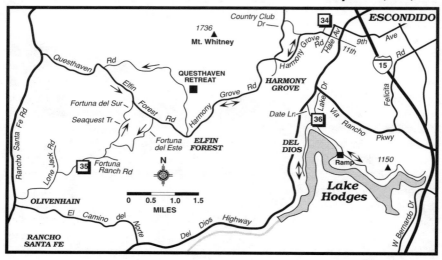

Trip 35. Fortuna Ranch Tour

Starting Point: Olivenhain (Encinitas)
GPS: Lat/Long 33° 4′ 2″, 117° 12′ 12″;
UTM 11S 481024mE 3658578mN
Distance: 5.5 miles
Elevation Gain: 850 feet
Riding Time: 1.5 hours
Road Conditions: Mostly rough dirt roads
Traffic Conditions: Light
Difficulty: **
Equipment: Mountain bikes required

This ride takes you into the outback, so to speak, between Encinitas and San Marcos. The area has so far escaped urban sprawl and remains somewhat undeveloped. There are a few steep climbs, but the views of the surrounding rural areas are worth the extra sweat.

To find the starting point, take the Encinitas Boulevard exit from Interstate 5 and head east. Turn left on Rancho Santa Fe Road, and later right on Lone Jack Road. Turn right on Fortuna Ranch Road and park alongside the road just before it turns to dirt.

Start pedaling east on the unpaved road and stay left at the sign for Fortuna Ranch Road. Construction in this area may lead to paving some of this road in the near future. At the next junction, keep left onto Canyon De Oro and head downhill. Soon you will jog right, then left, and cross over a dry stream bed that flows during wetter months. This section of the road gets rougher as it heads up the hill toward three broadcasting antennas.

At the top of the grade, follow the road left and continue climbing on unmarked Seaquest Trail. The hills are sparsely vegetated, but a few oak trees dot some hill tops in the distance. Soon you will pass the Seaquest Ranch and a small sign that asks riders to pass quietly. One hill seems to block the view of the ocean from this vantage point— perhaps the name Seaquest refers to this fact. At 1.4 miles, you reach the final summit, with a good view north and east into the Elfin Forest area.

Start your well-earned downhill, and stay right on the dirt road when you reach the bottom. You'll freewheel by the orderly rows of a lemon orchard as you continue your descent. Don't let the paved section fool you, as the road quickly turns back to dirt. There's a nice little grove of oaks ahead. At 2.0 miles, you'll hit pavement again. Now work your way up a hill on Fortuna del Sur to Elfin Forest Road.

Turn right on Elfin Forest Road and coast along a short downgrade. While climbing again, turn right on Fortuna del Este, just before the next crest. As you glide downhill, follow Fortuna del Este as it goes left and then climbs yet another hill. Watch for the interesting double-dome house and the LLAMA CROSSING sign and a number of llamas in the yard.

At 4.0 miles, the road reverts to dirt. A long, steep driveway to the left leads to the top of a hill to the east, where an enormous mansion sits some 500 feet above you. Keep straight on the dirt road. It drops downhill to cross a dry stream-bed and passes another mini-grove of oaks.

Rest your legs here, since the 0.2-mile climb up the next hill is very steep. Once at the top, the familiar broadcasting antennas will confirm than you have just completed a loop. Continue straight, downhill, and follow your earlier path back to the starting point.

Trip 36. Lake Hodges Tour

Starting Point: Escondido
GPS: Lat/Long 33° 4′ 39″, 117° 6′ 58″;
UTM 11S 489159mE 3659704mN
Distance: 15.5 miles
Elevation Gain: 350 feet
Riding Time: 2 hours
Road Conditions: Smooth to rough dirt roads
Difficulty: *
Equipment: Mountain bike

Imagine a hiking, biking, and equestrian trail extending from the Del Mar coast to the crest of a mountain pass near Julian. The proposed San Dieguito River Park Coast to Crest route will follow the San Dieguito River and Santa Ysabel Creek, with no highway crossings over the whole 55 miles. The first seven-mile segment of the San Dieguito River Park Trail is now open and ready for use. This ride will take you on a part of that trail following the shoreline of Lake Hodges. Lake Hodges is a man-made reservoir completed in 1918 by the San Dieguito Water District and purchased by the City of San Diego in 1925. Diverse natural plant communities including coastal sage scrub, chaparral, and riparian oak woodland surround it.

You begin at the north end of Lake Hodges, where Date Lane intersects Lake Drive. From Del Dios Highway, turn southeast on Date Lane to reach this intersection. From Via Rancho Parkway, turn south on Lake Drive to reach the same intersection. The parking lot there is open Wednesday, Saturday, and Sunday (dawn to dusk); otherwise just park your car alongside the road. A small store and restaurant are located nearby for refreshments after the ride. See Options for an alternate starting point off of I-15 and Via Rancho Parkway.

Lake Hodges

Start riding southeast on the road that hugs Lake Hodges' north shoreline. At 0.7 mile, pass a gate where fishermen line up in their vehicles at the crack of dawn, waiting to have a chance to try their luck. Ride on to a parking area and boat ramp, and continue southeast on a dirt road. Scattered oak and pepper trees and lots of buckwheat and laurel sumac grace the rolling hills on this side of the lake. In the warmer months, the prickly pear cacti covering some of the hillsides may be in bloom. The road ascends easily as it follows the shore of the lake and wraps around the base of 1150-foot Bernardo Mountain on your left.

After a rough, rutty, downhill section of road, you'll cross a shallow creek where oaks and sycamores provide cool shade. The road moves closer to the shoreline for a short while, and then runs into an abandoned section of highway that predates Interstate 15. When that road finally dead ends at a fence just short of I-15, a new section of paved trail continues to your right and under I-15. You can follow it on the other side of I-15 to a parking area and kiosk off of Sunset Drive. From here it's time to turn

around and retrace your path. You can amuse yourself on the way back by keeping an eye out for jackrabbits—several darted across our path.

When you return to your starting point, don't quit. Now explore the west end of the Coast to Crest trail, which skirts the little community of Del Dios. This will add another 4.5 miles or so (round trip). From the west end of the parking lot, continue through a eucalyptus-shaded park. Look for the little trail paralleling Lake Drive. Follow it through the oaks, and across several sharp little drainages.

When you come to a boat-launching ramp and the Hernandez Hideaway Restaurant, cross the parking area and follow the gated road signed COAST TO CREST. You continue to a picnic area and a dock where windsurfers launch their craft. Climb a small hill and follow the road to a gate with a road-closed sign. Here, the Coast to Crest route ends, for now, a fair distance short of the big concrete dam ahead. Return to your starting point the way you came, or else wend your way along the eclectic streets of Del Dios that parallel the Coast to Crest trail.

Options: Now that the Coast to Crest bike trail passes under I-15, an alternate starting point is the parking area at the end of Sunset Drive. Exit I-15 at Via Rancho Parkway and head a short distance east to Sunset Drive and turn right. Follow Sunset to the end and park. Of note is the Sikes Adobe Farmhouse, a state point of historic interest, just before you reach the trail staging area. The one-room adobe was constructed in 1870, just after Zenas Sikes and his wife Eliza moved to the site. They soon built onto the original adobe, the additional rooms made of wooden framing. A large porch surrounded the structure, and two large date palms graced the front—a typical Victorian statement. The farmhouse needs repairs and the River Park has begun the process of restoring it. When complete, the farmhouse will be open to the public for docent-led tours.

The Piedras Pintadas Trail on the south side of Lake Hodges is also part of the San Dieguito River Park and is a fun area to explore. Parking is available in or near the Rancho Bernardo Community Park on West Bernardo Drive, south of where it crosses Interstate 15. The trail is 3.8 miles round trip and a kiosk near the start explains the route. A nearby interpretive trail provides information about the Indians that inhabited this area. See http://www.sdrp.org for more information about the San Dieguito River Park.

Trip 37. San Pasqual - Highland Valley Loop

Starting Point: Escondido
GPS: Lat/Long 33° 4′ 40″, 117° 3′ 24″; UTM 11S 494701mE 3659720mN
Distance: 15 miles
Elevation Gain: 1100 feet
Riding Time: 2 hours
Road Conditions: Smooth roads with mostly narrow shoulders
Traffic Conditions: Heavy first 3 miles; otherwise light
Difficulty: **
Equipment: Any multi-geared bike

It's becoming more difficult to avoid heavily trafficked roads in the Escondido area, but this tour manages to do just that—except for the first three miles. You'll ride the hills overlooking Lake Hodges, and later visit the flat, verdant floor of San Pasqual Valley, an agricultural preserve.

A convenient place to begin is Kit Carson Park in south Escondido, just north of the North County Fair shopping center and the Via Rancho Parkway exit from Interstate 15. Begin by cycling south, then west past the shopping center entrances toward I-15. Your next move is to get on the southbound ramp of I-15 toward San Diego. Cross the overpass and maneuver over to the left turn lanes that funnel traffic onto the freeway. (You may also use the pedestrian WALK-DON'T WALK signals to get across Via Rancho Parkway and onto the ramp shoulder.)

Stay on the shoulder of I-15 for one mile, passing over an upper arm of Lake Hodges. Water levels in the lake fluctuate according to the local rainfall. Exit at the first opportunity—Pomerado Road. Bicycling on the freeway shoulder may be a new experience for many riders, but it is not an uncommon practice in San Diego County. Here and elsewhere, certain segments of freeway shoulders are officially open to bicycles

Coast to Crest Trail

and motor-driven cycles because of a lack of reasonable alternate routes. There are plans for a future bicycle and pedestrian bridge just west of the I-15 bridge that will make this route easier.

On Pomerado Road, continue east, once again passing over I-15. You'll pass a stone marker on the north side of the road commemorating nearby Mule Hill, which was associated with the 1846 Battle of San Pasqual. A visit to the San Pasqual Battlefield State Historic Park, six miles ahead on our route, will further enlighten you.

Turn left at the next intersection—Highland Valley Road—and leave the

traffic behind. In the next three miles along San Pasqual Valley, you'll pass several nurseries that specialize in products ranging from cut flowers to eucalyptus and palm seedlings.

Abruptly, the road begins a steep, winding ascent—400 feet of elevation gain along inclines as steep as 12 percent. Walk your bike if need be. After 0.6 mile, the worst is over. The road reaches a flat area appropriately named Highland Valley, and joins Bandy Canyon Road. Turn left, jog right then left, and begin a fast descent back into San Pasqual Valley.

When the road reaches the bottom of the valley, turn left on Ysabel Creek

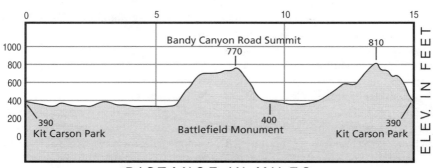

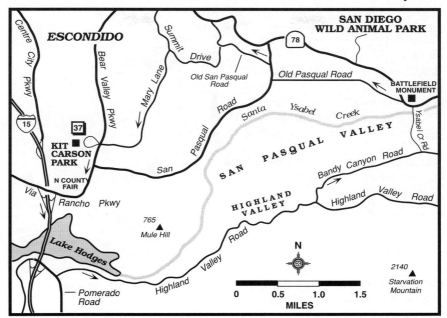

Road. It goes 0.6 mile north to join Highway 78 at the San Pasqual Battlefield Monument. Although Ysabel Creek Road is washed out where it crosses the normally dry, sandy bed of Santa Ysabel Creek, you can easily walk your bike through.

The monument is dedicated to the American soldiers who died in the Battle of San Pasqual in early December 1846. The legendary scout Kit Carson participated in this rather indecisive battle of the Mexican War. A new state historic park visitor center is located a quarter mile east of the monument along Highway 78.

From the monument, take the old highway (Old Pasqual Road) westward past pastures and cornfields. Turn right on busy San Pasqual Road, then turn left at the next road—Old San Pasqual Road. Pedal up the moderate incline and turn

left on Summit Drive. Continue on a mostly uphill grade, passing small avocado and citrus orchards and well-kept rural homes. A fine panorama of the San Pasqual Valley comes into view as you gain altitude.

A left turn on Mary Lane puts you on a course south, mostly downhill, along an undulating ridgeline. The view homes along this stretch overlook many miles of semi-rural and suburban development along the fringes of Escondido and San Diego. As Mary Lane veers west, a final downhill spin takes you straight back to Kit Carson Park.

Options: An eastern extension of this route might include a trip east on Highland Valley Road to the rural outskirts of Ramona. Narrow and winding Highway 78, the most direct route between Ramona and Escondido, is generally not recommended for cycling—there's too much fast-moving traffic.

A visit to the San Diego Wild Animal Park is worthwhile if you have a lot of time. Use the short stretch of Highway 78 to reach the entrance road. Bike racks are located near the ticket booths. The 1800-acre park, an annex of the San Diego Zoo, was designed to simulate the typical habitats of African wildlife. Not only does this spacious environment please tourists; it also stimulates many of the animals to reproduce as they would in the wild.

The San Dieguito River Park recently completed the Mule Hill/San Pasqual Valley Trail, a 9.4-mile-long trail for hikers, bicyclists and equestrians. It begins just east of I-15 on the north side of Lake Hodges and extends eastward through the San Pasqual Valley to Highway 78 at Bandy Canyon Road. The trail has interpretive signage about the historic resources in the valley, such as the Sikes Adobe Farmhouse, the Town of Bernardo, and Mule Hill. The trail is located in the agricultural preserve through the cooperation of the farmers

On Bandy Canyon Road

in the valley and the City of San Diego Water Department, which owns the valley. See http://www.sdrp.org for more information about the San Dieguito River Park.

Trip 38. Highland Valley Tour

Starting Point: Rancho Bernardo
GPS: Lat/Long 33° 1′ 23″, 117° 4′ 24″;
UTM 11S 493148mE 3653643mN
Distance: 27 miles
Elevation Gain: 2230 feet
Riding Time: 3.5 hours
Road Conditions: Smooth, paved roads with narrow to wide shoulders
Traffic Conditions: Light to moderately heavy
Difficulty: ***
Equipment: Any multi-geared bike

The fast-growing city of Poway has managed to balance its population

growth with aggressive preservation of recreation and wilderness areas. On this ride, skirting Poway's eastern fringe, you'll pass by several key open-space areas: Woodson Mountain, Iron Mountain, Lake Poway, and the Blue Sky Ecological Reserve. An early start on a weekend is best, as you'll avoid the commuter traffic that clogs Poway Road and Highway 67 during the week.

A good starting point for this ride is nearby Rancho Bernardo. You'll find

Trip 38

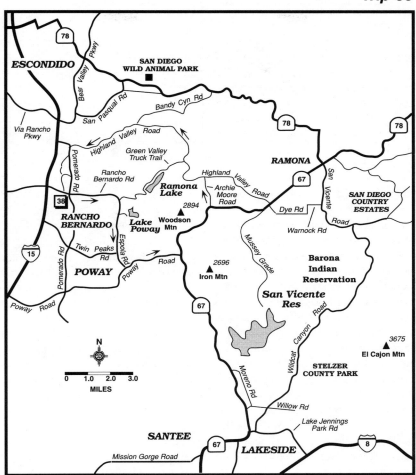

abundant parking space in or near the shopping area at the intersection of Rancho Bernardo Road and Bernardo Center Drive, just east of Interstate 15.

Ride east on Rancho Bernardo Road. Cross Pomerado Road and continue gradually uphill toward Poway's city limit and less suburban, more rural surroundings. The Stoneridge Country Club lies on your left, while straight ahead you'll spot the telecommunications towers atop distant Woodson Mountain. As

the road bends right, becoming Espola Road, you'll notice the entrance to Blue Sky Ecological Reserve—the Green Valley Truck Trail—on the left. A shortcut through here and up along the Ramona Reservoir used to be for those on mountain bikes—now it's hikers only. Espola Road, incidentally, was once the main route between Escondido and Lakeside by way of Poway. The Spanish-sounding "Es-Po-La" is really a contraction of the three city names.

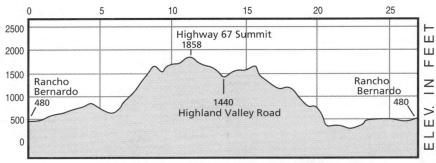

DISTANCE IN MILES

Continue south on Espola Road as it passes the entrance to the Lake Poway Recreation Area. There are grassy areas inside for lounging, but it's probably too early in the ride for that. Pseudo-country estates are rapidly taking over much of the area along Espola Road. After passing Poway High School, there's a 1.5-mile descent to Twin Peaks Road. Enjoy it, because some real climbing is about to begin—a 1030-foot gain in 2.4 miles.

When you reach Poway Road, turn left and continue climbing. Just beyond a eucalyptus grove on the left, you'll reach the top of the hill. Following this is a short, breath-catching glide to a T-intersection at Highway 67 (9.1 miles). Look up ahead (a little south of east) to spot Iron Mountain's summit. A multi-use trail leading to the top has recently been completed. Skilled mountain bikers may want to try the shorter branch of this trail, which starts within 50 yards of the T-intersection.

Turn left on Highway 67, and pick up a bit of speed before the next long climb. The road is busy, but newly improved with wide, smooth shoulders. As you make a sweeping turn to the right, Woodson Mountain (popularly known as Mount Woodson) comes into view on the

left. The rugged landscape hereabouts is densely covered in chaparral vegetation, with large slabs and boulders of light-gray granodiorite rock intervening. Exposure to the elements causes this rock to weather into huge spherical or ellipsoidal boulders with smooth surfaces—ideal for rock climbers searching for unique challenges. At the top of the grade, the road bends left and swoops down into the Santa Maria Valley, better known as the Ramona Valley.

On a right-hand curve at 12.4 miles, carefully pull into the left turn lane for Archie Moore Road, and make the turn. This road was recently paved, bringing housing development to the foot of scenic Woodson Mountain. You descend to Highland Valley Road, and turn left.

The next few miles of almost traffic-free road are great fun, with lots of turns and little ups and downs through the citrus and avocado groves. Here and there, you'll glide past live oaks and sycamores, and small ponds used for irrigation. Sight distance is short at times and the road is narrow, so be sure to stay close to the right edge of the road in case a car comes zooming around a curve. Also watch your speed on the curves, as the road is sandy in some places.

At mile marker 10, be ready for a 9+ percent downhill grade with sharp curves. You scream down to the valley floor below, where cattails and willows flourish on the margins of the fertile San Pasqual Valley. When the rain gods have been benevolent, the waters of Lake Hodges extend far into this valley. See the San Pasqual-Highland Valley Loop trip for information about a future multi-use trail through this valley.

Soon you'll dip to cross a streambed that may be wet in winter. A footbridge on the right can be used for the crossing if the water is too deep. Climb the little hill to Pomerado Road and turn left, joining busy traffic. At Mirasol Drive, 0.6 mile on, you can try a nice detour through the Rancho Bernardo Country Club—see Options. Otherwise stay straight. After passing the Rancho Bernardo Winery on the left, you'll reach the intersection of Rancho Bernardo Road. Turn right to return to your starting point.

Options: A somewhat longer but equally scenic way to complete this loop is to go through Ramona by way of Highways 67 and 78. The curvy, downhill stretch of Highway 78 northwest of Ramona through Clevenger Canyon is a real screamer. Heavy traffic on the highway can make this section less than fun, so you may want to try this alternate route only on a Sunday morning. Once you reach the bottom of the grade and emerge on the flatter terrain of San Pasqual Valley, you can turn left on Bandy Canyon Road and use it to connect with Highland Valley Road.

For the detour through the Rancho Bernardo Country Club, turn right off of Pomerado Road onto Mirasol Drive, and then left on Sintonte Drive. At the stop sign ahead, continue straight into the country club. Turn left at the next stop sign, and continue onto Bernardo Oaks Drive. This will take you to Rancho Bernardo Road, where you turn right to complete the ride.

Trip 39. Eucalyptus Hills

Starting Point: Lakeside
GPS: Lat/Long 32° 51′ 44″, 116° 56′ 31″; UTM 11S 505427mE 3635833mN
Distance: 4.5 miles
Elevation Gain: 600 feet
Riding Time: 45 minutes
Road Conditions: Smooth roads with narrow shoulders
Traffic Conditions: Light
Difficulty: **
Equipment: Any multi-geared bike

Eucalyptus Hills seems singularly isolated from the hustle and bustle of San Diego's metropolitan sprawl. Only one or two miles away from the eucalyptus-shaded hillsides and little ravines of this rural neighborhood, new subdivisions and industrial parks have covered the flatlands of Santee and Lakeside. Little or none of that is seen or heard from most parts of Eucalyptus Hills.

Some roads here are posted as private, so we've routed this short tour over public roads only. Nearly all of the elevation gain happens in the first two miles. You can begin at the corner of Riverside Drive and Palm Row Drive—one mile west of Lakeside's center—where plenty of parking space is available. Follow the arrows on our map, or choose your own variation of the route.

Eucalyptus tree

All the varieties of eucalyptus found here and elsewhere in the county are non-native. Originally from Australia, these trees were planted by the millions a century ago with the expectation that they would prove useful as a source of wood for fuel and construction. Their commercial value ultimately proved nil, but many an old eucalyptus grove today graces hillsides that would otherwise be treeless. Judging by the size of most of the eucalyptus here, they were planted after the turn of the twentieth century.

Residents of Eucalyptus Hills and other areas on the fringes of Lakeside and Santee have a fondness for horses. It isn't unusual to share the road with people on horseback as well as in cars.

Trips 39, 40

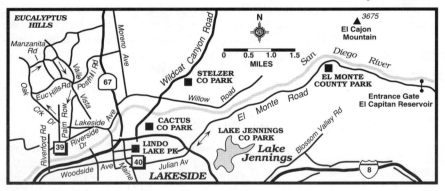

Trip 40. El Monte Road

Starting Point: Lakeside
GPS: Lat/Long 32° 51′ 28″, 116° 54′ 59″; UTM 11S 507820mE 3635342mN
Distance: 15 miles (round trip)
Elevation Gain: 280 feet
Riding Time: 1.5 hours
Road Conditions: Smooth roads with narrow shoulders
Traffic Conditions: Light to moderate

Difficulty: **
Equipment: Any multi-geared bike

If you don't like steep hills, you'll love El Monte Road. There's probably no other rural road in San Diego County (outside the desert) that can offer as long a stretch of nearly flat terrain without much traffic. The road follows the valley of the San Diego River, a place where the breeze seems to blow incessantly out of the west. Even though the turn-around point of this out-and-back ride is a little higher than the starting point, it is often easier to pedal out (eastbound) and harder to return.

During a Santa Ana condition, somewhat common in fall and early winter, the wind comes from the east and the opposite situation exists. Try this ride on a summer evening, on a dying breeze. For an hour or so before sunset, the river valley lies in purple shadow, and the sheer south granite face of El Cajon Mountain (or "El Capitan") overlooking the valley basks in a pinkish glow.

A good place to begin is Lindo Lake County Park, one block east of Maine Avenue, Lakeside's "main drag." Head east and south around the lake and the county park to Julian Avenue, and then go east about a mile to the intersection at Lake Jennings Park Road. Straight across is El Monte Road.

El Monte Road drops quickly to the San Diego River valley floor, and then very gradually ascends, staying close to the base of the hills on the south side. Initially a fertile plain almost a mile wide, the valley gradually narrows to form a U-shaped canyon. You'll pass a dairy (hold your nose), strawberry and vegetable farms, and horse corrals. The El Cajon Valley looked much like this before the post-World-War-II growth period.

After about four miles (from Lake Jennings Park Road) you'll come to El Monte County Park, which is open during daylight hours. The oak-shaded park is perfect for picnicking, and offers an impressive view of cliff-like El Capitan. On the road again, you resume the climb—a bit steeper now—and within two miles reach a gate and a turn-around. El Capitan Reservoir lies ahead, open on certain days for boating and fishing.

San Diego River Valley

Trip 41. Harbison Canyon - Crest Loop

Starting Point: El Cajon
GPS: Lat/Long 32° 47′ 16″, 116° 55′ 0″;
UTM 11S 507791mE 3627576mN
Distance: 16.3 miles
Elevation Gain: 1440 feet
Riding Time: 2 hours
Road Conditions: Smooth roads with
narrow to wide shoulders
Traffic Conditions: Moderate; heavy on
Dehesa Road
Difficulty: ***
Equipment: Any multi-geared bike with
low gears

The adjacent communities of Harbison Canyon and Crest are separated by not much more than one mile of horizontal distance, but 700 feet of elevation. This ride includes a challenging climb up Mountain View Road—the road connecting the two. The rest of the ride is, thankfully, mostly downhill. Note that the addition of the Sycuan Casino has increased traffic significantly on Dehesa Road. You may want to save this ride for early on a Sunday morning.

A good place to begin is the intersection of Granite Hills Drive and Dehesa Road on the southeast edge of El Cajon. Ample parking is available along nearby Washington Avenue. Head east on Dehesa Road, climbing for about one

mile to a low summit. A breezy downgrade follows, with a panoramic view of the Sweetwater River Valley below. The bright green patch ahead is the Singing Hills Golf Course.

After reaching Willow Glen Road at the bottom, Dehesa Road assumes a near-level, eastward course along the north side of the river valley. Much of the valley floor has become a trap for sediment, and a sand-and-gravel quarry is located here to exploit this resource.

Soon Dehesa Road swings north, leaving the Sweetwater River Valley, and starts climbing slightly. Stay straight (on what is now called Harbison Canyon Road) where Dehesa Road turns abruptly east toward Japatul Road and Alpine. After more climbing along a shadeless slope, the road enters the narrow portals of shady Harbison Canyon. For the next mile, you'll find the small, rustic community of Harbison Canyon, whose growth has been kept in check by a scarcity of building sites.

Look for Frances Drive on the left. This becomes Mountain View Road within a couple of blocks. As you labor up the grade toward Crest, try to get a

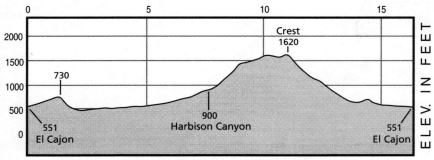

Dehesa Road

glimpse of the panorama widening behind you. Mountain View Road assumes a more moderate gradient near the top, dips down momentarily, and then climbs to a final summit. The hilltop community of Crest unfolds to the south. On clear days, a wide expanse of the Pacific Ocean can be seen from here. Nancy Jane County Park, half a mile south on La Cresta Boulevard, is a pleasant destination if you want to poke around Crest a bit.

Our way continues west down La Cresta Road. The downhill ride is a very fast one, but so is the traffic, so be very alert. After a few minutes, you arrive at Greenfield Drive. Turn left and pedal 0.6 mile uphill to Madison Avenue. Turn right and glide down 0.3 mile to Granite Hills Drive. Make a left there and follow the remaining 1.5 miles of Granite Hills Drive as it curves back to the starting point.

Trips 41, 42, 43, 44

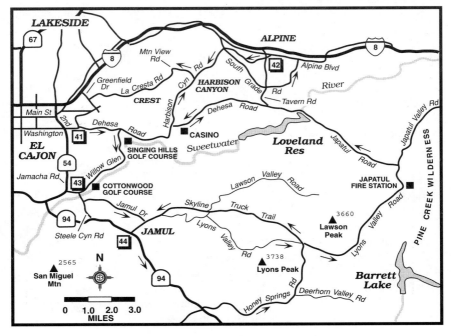

Trip 42. Alpine Tour

Starting Point: Alpine
GPS: Lat/Long 32° 51' 8", 116° 48' 35";
UTM 11S 517804mE 3634715mN
Distance: 16.7 miles
Elevation Gain: 1550 feet
Riding Time: 2 hours
Road Conditions: Smooth roads with
narrow shoulders
Traffic Conditions: Light to moderate;
heavy on Dehesa Road
Difficulty: ***
Equipment: Any multi-geared bike

The rapidly growing foothill town of Alpine once displayed a sign along the main highway boasting "Best Climate in the USA by Government Report." Apparently the town boosters got what they wanted—an influx of new residents. Many have moved here for relatively affordable housing, and almost all commute to El Cajon or San Diego, 15 to 30 minutes away by way of Interstate 8. Still, the point about nice weather is well taken. Summer's a bit hot much of the time, but most days in fall, winter, and spring have sunny skies and near-perfect temperatures.

Unlike most trips in this book, this one begins with a steady drop and concludes with a substantial climb. If this isn't to your liking, try starting at the low point on this ride—the intersection of Harbison Canyon Road and Dehesa Road. The addition of the Sycuan Casino has increased traffic significantly on Dehesa Road. This ride may be best traversed on a Sunday morning.

Our starting point is the intersection of Alpine Boulevard and Arnold Way in Alpine's older and quaint business district. Follow Arnold Way across Tavern Road and down a winding grade through an attractive rural residential area. At the bottom of the grade, turn left on Harbison Canyon Road. New subdivisions fill part of the valley ahead.

The road soon pitches downward along the bottom of narrow Harbison Canyon into the town of the same name. Cruising along in an automobile, you might easily miss many of the unique sights, sounds and smells of this small community. As a cyclist, you can savor the atmosphere of this cool, wooded canyon to the fullest. Oak-shaded Old Ironsides County Park, on the left, is a good place for a picnic. See Options below for an interesting detour through the town.

Continue down the canyon to Dehesa Road. Turn left there, and shift into the gear that best suits the long, moderate incline ahead. As you gain altitude, the hillsides become steeper. The road snakes up the north side of a dry canyon, with slabs of granitic rock and khaki-colored brush forming a rugged tapestry on both walls.

Make a sharp left turn when you reach the **Y**-intersection with Tavern Road. After further climbing, turn right onto South Grade Road. This gently rolling road takes you past many of Alpine's newer and more expensive houses and rural properties. When you reach Alpine Boulevard, turn left and coast two miles back into Alpine's town center.

Options: To see a bit more of the interesting backroads of Harbison Canyon, turn left onto East Noakes Street at Old Ironsides Park. Stay right on Silverbrook Drive and wind your way through an area of eclectic residences shaded by the many oak trees in the area. Turn right at Collier Way to return to Harbison Canyon Road.

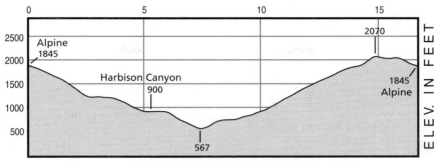

Trip 43. Lyons Valley - Japatul Loop

Starting Point: Rancho San Diego
GPS: Lat/Long 32° 44′ 44″, 116° 55′ 0″;
UTM 11S 507807mE 3622891mN
Distance: 40 miles
Elevation Gain: 3700 feet
Riding Time: 4.5 hours
Road Conditions: Smooth roads with narrow to wide shoulders
Traffic Conditions: Light to moderate
Difficulty: ****
Equipment: Any multi-geared bike

A few miles east of San Diego's outlying suburbs you can find some of the nicest back country in all of southern California. The secluded Lee, Lyons, Japatul, and Dehesa valleys are separated from the urban sprawl by steep, intervening ridges. Access to these secluded haunts is by way of winding mountain roads that serve the relatively few local residents, as well as occasional intrepid visitors on bikes.

Much of the higher country—the slopes and peaks—along this route are part of Cleveland National Forest. This public land, mostly unsuitable for agricultural use, remains essentially in a natural state. Chaparral, which is a mixture of tough, drought-resistant shrubs, makes up the bulk of this unspoiled landscape. When in bloom during late winter and early spring, the various kinds of chaparral plants exude an almost intoxicating odor.

The best place to begin this loop route is at its low point—Cottonwood Golf Course—that is now being almost swallowed by the burgeoning Rancho San Diego development. Curbside parking is available in a subdivision along Willow Glen Road opposite Steele Canyon Road.

Head east on Steele Canyon Road for about 0.5 mile, then turn left on Jamul Drive. This is a steeper, but quieter alternative to busy Highway 94. Before long, housing developments—and the wide road shoulder—are left behind. The road twists up a narrow canyon (Mexican Canyon) shaded by live oaks and sycamores. After about two miles of fairly steady climbing, a very steep pitch takes you out of the canyon bottom and up to the intersection of Lyons Valley Road. Turn left there.

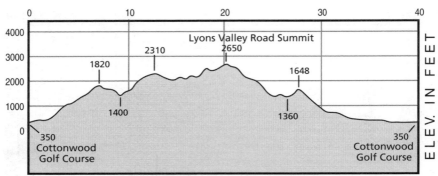

DISTANCE IN MILES

After another mile, Lyons Valley Road veers right, while the main road—a newer, high-speed route called Skyline Truck Trail—continues straight. Skyline Truck Trail is a more direct way to reach our destination of Lyons Valley, but the long, boring, and steep grades are demoralizing when pedaling in the uphill direction. We recommend the road less traveled—the old Lyons Valley Road.

Lyons Valley Road ascends gradually over the next 2.5 miles. After a horseshoe bend, the narrow ribbon of asphalt twists and turns along a hillside with a great view of the Jamul area below. After passing scattered oaks, scrub brush, and many new custom homes, you finally attain an 1820-foot summit. Stay straight at the next intersection and coast down into oak-dotted Lee Valley. Up ahead lies a cluster of bouldered peaks, including the massive Lyons Peak, topped by a fire lookout tower.

At the east end of Lee Valley, the road drops abruptly, goes sharply left (slow down before reaching this curve!), crosses the bottom of a small ravine, and begins a devilish climb to a notch in the mountains ahead. Lyons Valley lies beyond the top of that steep grade.

Amid the shade-giving oaks in Lyons Valley, you'll find a fire station (water is usually available here) and a small store. Continue east (straight) at the Honey Springs Road/Skyline Truck Trail intersection, and begin a breezy descent. Most of what lies ahead is in Cleveland National Forest.

After the downgrade, the road curves northeast, passing well below the granite-ribbed slopes of Lawson and Gaskill peaks to the west, and above a series of grassy valleys to the east used chiefly for cattle grazing.

Then, a long upgrade takes you to the turnoff for the Japatul Fire Station. The station is 0.5 mile away, with water usually available there. Below and to the east, but mostly hidden from this vantage point, is the gorge containing Pine Valley Creek. The roadless area along the creek—Pine Creek Wilderness—has recently earned important legal protection against any kind of development. Farther east, another prominent geographic feature—Corte Madera Mountain—punctuates the horizon.

Just beyond the next broad summit (2650 feet) you descend slightly to join Japatul Road. Turn left, and enjoy an almost uninterrupted five miles of downgrade. The usual breezes out of the west may temper some of the excitement by slowing you down quite a bit.

Lyons Valley Road

At the bottom of that grade, Japatul Road curves around the upper margins of Loveland Reservoir—often dry and dotted with the skeletons of dead trees. After crossing the Sweetwater River on the new, wide bridge, the road climbs up the side of a ridge and begins another long descent.

When you come to a major road fork—Tavern Road on the right, Dehesa Road on the left—take the left. More downgrade lies ahead. When you reach the **T**-intersection below Harbison Canyon, turn left (you actually remain on Dehesa Road that way). You now follow the bank of the Sweetwater River, passing some uninteresting sand and gravel pits. On weekdays, big trucks use this stretch of road, but the shoulder is wide.

The scenery improves at Singing Hills Golf Course. A line of olive trees defines the perimeter of the course for a mile or so. Don't miss the left turn onto Willow Glen Road. The last four miles are quite flat, but you'll have to fight the usual headwinds blowing up the valley of the Sweetwater River.

Options: To go from San Diego to Descanso—the gateway to the mountain country of the Cuyamacas and Lagunas—many cyclists like either the Dehesa Road/Japatul Road route, or the Lyons Valley/Japatul Road route. Both are somewhat more scenic, but longer and more difficult alternatives to the more common route that parallels Interstate 8 (see the Getting Out of San Diego Appendix).

Trip 44. Honey Springs - Skyline Loop

Starting Point: Jamul
GPS: Lat/Long 32° 43′ 0″, 116° 52′ 30″;
UTM 11S 511714mE 3619689mN
Distance: 21.5 miles
Elevation Gain: 2700 feet
Riding Time: 3.5 hours
Road Conditions: Smooth roads with narrow to wide shoulders
Traffic Conditions: Light to moderate
Difficulty: ***
Equipment: Any multi-geared bike

So far and yet so close. Only minutes away from the frenetic pace of the city, rolling meadows lie open to the sky, and boulder-studded hills form a backdrop akin to the interior of some sleepy Aegean island. Aloof, ethereal Lyons Peak, rising almost 4000 feet above sea level, dominates the viewscape.

The town of Jamul, the focus of this region and the starting point for this ride,

is conveniently located just 25 minutes (by auto) east of downtown San Diego via Highway 94. You can start from the shopping center at the corner of Jefferson Road and Highway 94. Except for private residences, there's no water along the route, so be sure to pick up water or beverages before you begin the ride.

Start by heading east on Highway 94. Like most of San Diego County, this area receives scant annual rainfall, most of it coming during the winter months. In the early spring, the broad valleys become amphitheaters of tall grasses, and the hillsides wear a cloak of bright green chaparral vegetation. During the remainder of the year, the grass dries to a yellow or brown color, and the chaparral fades to gray-green.

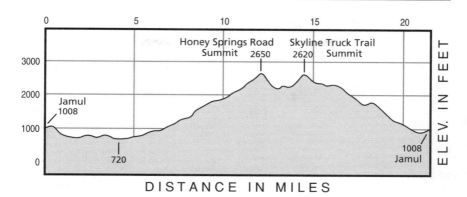

DISTANCE IN MILES

Five miles out from Jamul, turn left on Honey Springs Road. Next comes a climb that will separate the expert from the novice riders. The one and only hope here is a push from the prevailing wind out of the southwest. On hot days this tailwind can be a curse in disguise, as one's forward motion cancels out the fanning effect of the breeze.

A small, flat stretch shaded by live oaks about four miles up the grade is a good place to rest. The grade becomes steeper before leveling at the next summit. On your left is the rocky summit of Lyons Peak, topped by a fire lookout tower—one of the few remaining active lookouts in San Diego County.

Just past mile marker 17 is the Deerhorn Fire Station with water always available from a spigot out front if you need to refill your water bottles. After reaching the summit, roll down the steep grade toward Lyons Valley and keep straight at the intersection of Lyons Valley Road. Skyline Truck Trail, the generously wide road ahead, is a ridge-running route offering you the easiest passage back to Jamul. Years ago, this was a dirt road suitable only for truck and 4-wheel-drive traffic, hence its name. From the summit area of Skyline

Truck Trail you can look north across a promenade of mountain ranges varying in color and texture, culminating with the wave-shaped form of Cuyamaca Peak.

The final downhill takes you very swiftly back to the edge of Jamul. Near the bottom of the grade, Lyons Valley Road angles in from the south, and the road you travel now assumes that name. Soon after, Jefferson Road slants to the left, offering a short cut to the business district of Jamul.

Options: Two recommended side roads along this route are Deerhorn Valley Road, about 3 miles each way, and Lawson Valley Road, 5.5 miles each way. Both roads involve some challenging ups and downs. Lawson Valley is perhaps San Diego County's most secluded rural residential area—worthy in itself as a destination for an out-and-back ride from Jamul.

As an alternative to the Skyline Truck Trail segment of the ride, you can opt to follow Lyons Valley Road—more scenic, but more curvy and difficult than Skyline Truck Trail in the Lyons Valley-Japatul Loop trip.

Trip 45. Otay Lakes Tour

Starting Point: Southwestern College
(Chula Vista)
GPS: Lat/Long 32° 38′ 30″, 116° 59′ 36″;
UTM 11S 500618mE 3611378mN
Distance: 32 miles (round trip)
Elevation Gain: 800 feet
Riding Time: 3 hours
Road Conditions: Smooth roads with
mostly wide shoulders
Traffic Conditions: Light to moderate
Difficulty: ***
Equipment: Any multi-geared bike

Otay Lakes Road has long been a
favorite of bicyclists from Chula Vista
and the South Bay area. In fact, it is
the only paved, rural road conveniently accessible to the south end of the
county. Now, however, big changes are
underway on the east edge of Chula Vista. The East Lake development, which
will eventually house 30,000 people,
is beginning to swallow the empty, rolling hills that once stretched unbroken to
the edge of Upper and Lower Otay lakes.
Another future development in the area,
called Otay Ranch, could add 100,000
people by the year 2025.

West of the lakes, Otay Lakes Road
is becoming a wide, busy thoroughfare.
East of the lake, there's not much change
as yet.

Southwestern College (on Otay
Lakes Road between Telegraph Canyon
Road and H Street) is a good place to
start this exploration of both new suburbia and wide-open country. Head south
down the little hill to the Telegraph Canyon Road intersection—turn left there
and ride east on a gentle upgrade.

East Lake

About the time Lower Otay Lake comes into view, turn right on Wueste Road. The out-and-back excursion ahead takes you past the U.S. Olympic Training Center. Wueste Road follows the same contour for nearly three miles, bending around several arms of the lake. In early spring, the green hills to the west contrast pleasingly with the dark blue water of the lake; in summer this contrast is stark—gold against blue.

When you return to Otay Lakes Road, turn right. You swing around a north arm of the lake, catching sight of the old concrete dam of Upper Otay Lake to the left.

You ride east, following a shallow east arm of Lower Otay Lake, and then pass over Dulzura Creek (the main feeder stream of the lake). The road has been widened and smoothed out—very pleasant for cycling. On your right you'll spot the San Diego Air Sports Center, specializing in glider launching and skydiving. The pillowy San Ysidro Mountains (better known as Otay Mountain) rise behind the tiny airfield.

In the next two miles, Otay Lakes Road follows the south bank of Dulzura Creek, curving and climbing gradually. A dense strip of riparian vegetation, mostly willows, accompanies the creek. The tangled vegetation exudes a unique kind of humid odor. Hawks often soar overhead, scouting for rodents that thrive along the banks of the creek.

Thousand Trails resort is next. There you'll find a store open to the public. Two more miles of narrower road lead to Highway 94—the place to turn around and head back to Chula Vista.

When you're back in the East Lake development again, circle back to the starting point by way of East Lake

Trips 45, 46

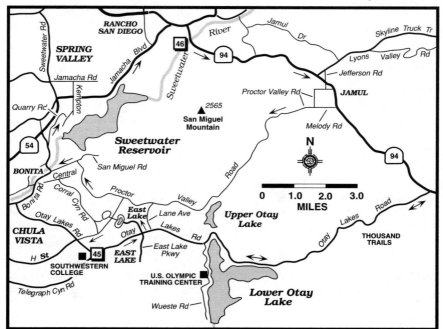

Parkway and H Street. Along the way you'll loop around shallow East Lake. It's of artificial origin, but apparently realistic enough to attract a fair share of waterfowl.

Options: Upon reaching Highway 94, you can extend your ride in any of three directions. East on Highway 94 takes you along many miles of winding road toward Dulzura, Tecate and Campo. A jog left (west) on Highway 94, then right on Honey Springs Road takes you up to

Lyons Valley (see Lyons Valley-Japatul Loop and Honey Springs-Skyline Loop trips) and ultimately to Descanso and the Cuyamaca and Laguna mountains. West on Highway 94 takes you through Jamul to Spring Valley, where you can circle back to the starting point on mostly heavily trafficked highways. An alternative way to loop back is to take Proctor Valley Road (a graded dirt road) west and south from Jamul (see Around San Miguel Mountain trip below).

Trip 46. Around San Miguel Mountain

Starting Point: Rancho San Diego
GPS: Lat/Long 32° 44′ 5″, 116° 56′ 25″;
UTM 11S 505591mE 3621681mN
Distance: 25 miles
Elevation Gain: 1800 feet
Riding Time: 2.5 hours
Road Conditions: Graded dirt road; paved roads and highways with narrow to wide shoulders
Traffic Conditions: Light to heavy
Difficulty: ***
Equipment: Mountain bike

Cone-shaped San Miguel looms large from the East County communities of Spring Valley, Rancho San Diego, and Jamul. This circumnavigation of the mountain includes a long stretch of graded dirt road on the mountain's "back" side, and a cruise on pavement down busy Highways 94 and 54 through the emerging suburbs. An early start on a Sunday morning is emphatically recommended. Heavy traffic on parts of this route makes for a rather unenjoyable time otherwise.

You can begin at the west end of the old, steel Sweetwater River bridge next

to Highway 94, where parking space is available. The old bridge was saved for use by pedestrians and cyclists when the new bridge was constructed in the late 1980s.

Ride east on Highway 94, gradually then more steeply uphill, to the main shopping center in Jamul, 4.5 miles away. Make a right on Jefferson Road, a right on Maxfield Road, and a left on Proctor Valley Road. After 0.7 mile, you'll have to make a right turn to stay on Proctor Valley Road. After another mile or so of rural housing, the road turns to dirt and there's nothing but wide-open space ahead as far as your eyes can see. In 20 years, however, some 100,000 people may inhabit what you see spread before you. By then, Proctor Valley Road could well be a 6- or 8-lane highway.

Near Upper Otay Lake, the road turns east, climbs for a while and begins skirting the new East Lake development on the east fringe of Chula Vista. The road turns to pavement as you pass through several areas of new housing.

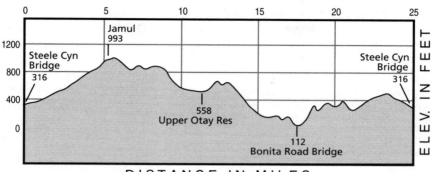

DISTANCE IN MILES

Turn right on Mount San Miguel Road, then left again on Proctor Valley Road. In a few hundred yards you will be back on the dirt again where you start a curving descent leading down toward San Miguel Road, where pavement resumes. Turn left on San Miguel and continue to Bonita Road. Make a right, cross over the Sweetwater River on a narrow bridge, and make a right at the next intersection—Sweetwater Road. Ride 0.7 mile to Quarry Road and turn right. As you start climbing up this old 2-lane road, you'll spot the venerable Sweetwater dam plugging a canyon on the right. When completed in 1888, the 90-foot-high dam was the highest dam in the United States. Further work raised it by another 20 feet. By today's standards, it looks rather small.

Continue over a summit and down to the big parking lot that serves as a swap meet on the weekends. Swing to the right, staying on Quarry Road, and then turn left when you reach Lakeview

Avenue. Bear left again when you reach Kempton Street two blocks later.

Continue north on Kempton to Jamacha Boulevard (Highway 54) and turn right. There are bike lanes along this busy road, which soon breaks out of the tacky suburban sprawl and skirts the north shore of Sweetwater Reservoir. You'll pass the huge Pointe Resort development on both sides of the highway just past the reservoir.

After reaching a low summit, you coast down to Campo Road (Highway 94). Make a right there, coast another half mile, and make a right again to return to the old Sweetwater River bridge.

Options: After reaching the new developments near the end of Proctor Valley Road, left on Hunte Parkway will take you to Otay Lakes Road and Olympic Parkway where the U.S. Olympic Training Center is located. See the Otay Lakes Tour ride.

Trip 47. Palomar Mountain Tour

Starting Point: Highway 76 below
Palomar Mountain
GPS: Lat/Long 33° 15′ 10″, 116° 47′ 28″;
UTM 11S 519448mE 3679141mN
Distance: 27.5 miles
Elevation Gain: 3300 feet
Riding Time: 3.5 hours
Road Conditions: Smooth roads with
narrow shoulders
Traffic Conditions: Light to moderate
Difficulty: ****
Equipment: Any multi-geared bike

Palomar Mountain, well-known for
its astronomical observatory, also happens to be an idyllic mountain play-
ground for picnicking, fishing, hiking
and camping. Thousands of band-tailed
pigeons once graced these slopes with
their nests, suggesting to the early Spanish settlers the name "Palomar" or "pi-
geon roost." A smaller population of
these birds still makes their home here.

Two spectacular paved roadways ascend to Palomar Mountain—South
Grade Road and East Grade Road. Both
roads begin along Highway 76 and intersect at the top of the mountain, thus a
circle trip up and down the slopes is possible. South Grade Road is the more
steep and winding of the two; so we suggest you pedal up this first, saving a

carefree, freewheeling descent for the
end of the trip.

A good place to park and begin this
tour is San Luis Rey Picnic Ground, on
Highway 76 about two miles west of
Lake Henshaw. The road into the picnic
area is normally open during the daylight
hours, but if it's closed, there's still plenty of roadside parking space outside.

Begin by riding west on the highway,
parallel to the San Luis Rey River.
Steady releases of water from Lake Henshaw usually keep this part of the river
flowing exuberantly. By the time you
reach the entrance to the La Jolla Indian
Reservation Campground, about four
miles from the start, the road has already
turned uphill. The grade steepens and the
road veers north away from the river
canyon in order to gain a foothold on a
gently rolling terrace studded with oaks.
Down below you can see why the highway has left the course of the river: a
narrow, rock-ribbed gorge is visible
downstream.

One mile after topping out on the terrace, you'll come to the turnoff for Palomar Mountain—South Grade Road. An
old name for this road is "Highway to

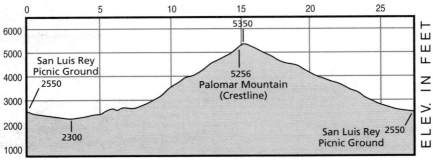

South Grade Road

the Stars"—an entirely appropriate description of its path to earthly as well as celestial heights. In just under seven miles you'll climb 2500 feet on a remarkably constant 7 percent grade.

The roadway curves incessantly, affording an ever-changing view of the lowlands below. Elevation signs every 1000 vertical feet keep you apprised of your progress. It's nice to take the mind off the vigor (pain?) of the climb by noticing how the vegetation changes with altitude. The live oaks, grasslands and chaparral of the lower slopes of the mountain are almost completely replaced by a thick forest of mixed deciduous and coniferous trees by the time you reach the top. The mixed forest includes incense-cedar, which looks much like a redwood tree; big-cone Douglas-fir, characterized by long, wand-like branches; Coulter pine, characterized by long needles and ponderous cones; white fir, prized as a classic Christmas-type tree; and black oak, a deciduous tree that is responsible for most of the autumnal color in these mountains.

Wherever the road curves around the deeper ravines and creeks, you'll also see the white alder tree. Near the wide intersection at the top of the grade (sometimes called Crestline) you'll find a market and cafe. This is the jumping-off place for side trips to the observatory and state park on Palomar Mountain, which we describe in detail below. Our route back down the mountain, though, goes east toward Lake Henshaw on East Grade Road.

East Grade Road climbs for about 0.5 mile to a summit with a breathtaking view west and south; then it starts to pitch downward. This is the beginning of a delightful descent which continues almost uninterrupted for the remaining 12 miles of the ride. Occasional use of the brakes and a few pedal strokes here and there are all that are needed as you glide along open hillsides, through shady wooded areas, and across two broad

Palomar Observatory

meadows. Near the bottom of the grade, a fabulous view of Lake Henshaw and the big basin surrounding it—Valle de San Jose—opens up.

When you reach Highway 76, turn right and continue coasting back toward your starting point. The soft whisper of the San Luis Rey River will accompany you all the way.

Options: From Crestline, you can take Canfield Road (Highway to the Stars) north to Observatory and Fry Creek campgrounds, and beyond to the Palomar Observatory visitors parking lot. The round trip to and from the observatory is nine miles with a total elevation gain of 1100 feet. The immense white dome at the observatory houses the

200-inch-diameter Hale reflector telescope, one of the country's biggest. From 9 a.m. to 4 p.m., you can get a view of the 500-ton precision instrument from a glass-walled visitor's gallery, and also visit a museum nearby.

West from Crestline by way of East Grade Road, you'll find beautiful Palomar Mountain State Park. Ride 2.5 miles to reach the entrance booth and Silver Crest Picnic Area. If time and energy allow, visit Boucher Hill and Doane Pond, both accessible by paved road. On the clearest days, Boucher Hill offers a view of the coastal strip and a wide arc of ocean horizon. Doane Pond, popular as a fishing hole, has picnic grounds along its shoreline.

Trips 47, 48, 49, 50

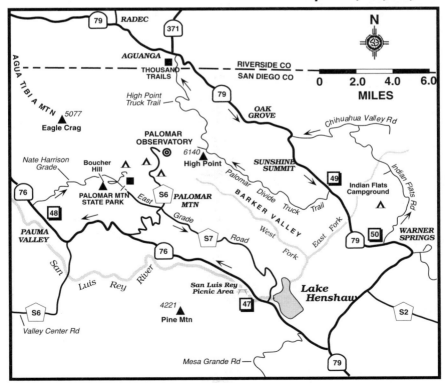

Trip 48. Nate Harrison Grade

Starting Point: Pauma Valley
GPS: Lat/Long 33° 18′ 10″, 116° 58′ 36″;
UTM 11S 502161mE 3684673mN
Distance: 30 miles
Elevation Gain: 4850 feet
Riding Time: 5 hours
Road Conditions: Graded dirt road;
smooth, paved roads and highways
with narrow to wide shoulders.
Traffic Conditions: Light on Nate Harrison
Grade; otherwise moderate
Difficulty: ****
Equipment: Mountain bike

If either of the two paved roads up Palomar Mountain (see the Palomar Mountain Tour) are too tame for you, then the relentlessly steep Nate Harrison Grade should please you well. This graded dirt road climbs almost 4000 feet in less than 10 miles, carving its way up the sun-struck, south-facing slopes. Near the top, you get to trade the heat and wide-ranging views for a beautiful passage through a cool oak-and-conifer forest.

The circa-1900 Nate Harrison Grade, originally a wagon route, predated the "Highway to the Stars" (a.k.a. South Grade Road) by at least 35 years. The road was named after Nathan Harrison, a freed slave who homesteaded a small ranch part of the way up the incline. Nate

graciously provided water for thirsty horses and travelers coming up the mountain. Over the years, Nate's road has been widened and the switchbacks rounded off, but its wild character remains today for anyone on wheels of any kind.

It's easiest to start at Pauma Valley, the low point, where you'll find a general store and not much else. This starting point is on Highway 76, 14.5 miles east of Interstate 15 and 1.5 miles east of Cole Grade Road.

Ride west on 76 for 1 mile to reach the foot of the Nate Harrison Grade. Then pedal uphill—on pavement at first—through orderly rows of sweet-smelling citrus trees. The Pauma Indian Reservation lies just west of here. *Pauma* is an Indian word meaning "place of little water," which is evident in the area's sparse native vegetation—mostly white sage at this elevation.

All too soon the incline becomes steeper and the pavement ends. The relentless climb brings you to successively higher vantage points where you can look down on the patchwork quilt of citrus orchards below. After about 5 miles, a short spur road on the right provides

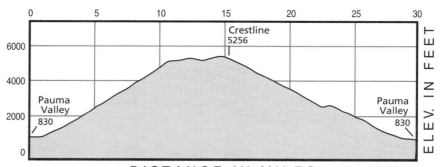

DISTANCE IN MILES

Nate Harrison Grade

the excuse you need to take a breather. It leads to the edge of a steep ravine with a great view to the south.

As you climb on, the aromatic sage-scrub vegetation draping the lower mountainside gives way to oaks. Higher still, the oaks are joined by tall firs and cedars, and you reach the boundary of Palomar Mountain State Park. Soon, you're back on pavement again, enjoying the distinctly cooler breeze and the silky smooth feel of the now more flat road.

Continue straight through the park, exiting the main entrance to join East Grade Road. You then roll along the southern rim of the mountain to Crestline—the main Palomar Mountain crossroads. Perhaps a stop at Mother's Kitchen, on the left, for a fruit smoothie is in order.

From this point on, you're entitled to cash in on gravity's debt to you.

There's 4400 feet of descent ahead—entirely on pavement. You begin right away with the descent on South Grade Road. Watch your downhill speed—some of the turns are sharper than they look and span more than 180° of curvature.

Keep straight when South Grade Road merges with Highway 76, and continue the relentless coast down past Rincon Springs to your starting point in Pauma Valley. On arrival, you'll have spun the crank only a few times over the last 14 miles of travel.

Trip 49. East Palomar Mountain Loop

Starting Point: Near Warner Springs
GPS: Lat/Long 33° 21' 3", 116° 44' 13";
UTM 11S 524468mE 3690027mN
Distance: 37.0 miles
Elevation Gain: 4100 feet
Riding Time: 6 hours
Road Conditions: Graded and rough dirt
roads; smooth, paved highway with
narrow shoulder
Traffic Conditions: Moderate on
Highway 79; otherwise light
Difficulty: ****
Equipment: Mountain bikes only

If you're looking for another challenging, dirt-road route up Palomar Mountain, this is it. Not quite as steep as the Nate Harrison Grade (see the Nate Harrison Grade trip), it climbs the drier eastern slopes, offering stunning views of Lake Henshaw to the south and the San Jacinto and San Bernardino mountains to the north. If you can summon up a bit of extra strength on Palomar's "High Point," you can climb 91 steps to the top of a 60-foot fire tower to take advantage of an even better view.

During summer the trip can be a two- or three-water-bottle effort, so prepare accordingly. Usually, water is not available until you reach Aguanga, by which time most of the effort of the trip has been expended. Winter may bring snow to the higher slopes several times yearly, rendering this route practically impassable for up to a week at a time.

You begin at the foot of Palomar Divide Road (signed 9S07), near mile marker 41.9 on Highway 79. This is 6.5 miles northwest of Warner Springs. Park in the clearing just off the highway and start riding up the dirt road. Sometimes the gate is shut—road closed to motor vehicles—but self-propelled travelers may proceed. The somewhat tedious

climb is relieved by the ever-widening view and (in springtime) by roadside carpets of lupine and other wildflowers.

After nearly 6 miles, look for a small, round water tank on the right—a source of water for fire fighting. Around the next bend you'll notice a large paved area that collects rainwater for the tank. Farther up the road you may notice a small battered rock cabin.

At 7.4 miles, Halfway Truck Trail intersects on the right, and you'll probably wish you were more than half finished with the ascent by then. Ahead a bit farther is the trailhead for the Barker Valley Trail, which descends to the West Fork of the San Luis Rey River. When you reach the large clump of oaks you've probably been eyeing on the horizon, at 11.9 miles, reward yourself with a siesta in the shade and a bite to eat. This pleasant spot is known as Deer Flats. A north branch of the Barker Valley Trail comes up to this point.

The road to High Point intersects on the left at 12.0 miles. For a worthwhile side trip, follow it up through oaks and pines, and veer left on the road to the lookout (straight-ahead lies Palomar Observatory, land off limits to the public).

Back on the main Palomar Divide Road (now signed Oak Grove Road), you begin the exhilarating descent that will take you back down to Highway 79 at Aguanga. Soon Oak Grove Road veers right to a locked gate, but High Point Truck Trail continues left. The road surface on this side is not as smooth as on the way up, so watch your downhill speed. During the late spring, yerba santa bushes color the hillsides purple on this side of the mountain.

At 23.5 miles, you'll end the long, downhill stretch by crossing a usually dry streambed. Keep straight when you reach pavement—this is the right-of-way for both the Thousand Trails campground and High Point Road. When you reach Highway 79, you probably won't mind detouring left 0.5 mile for a cold soda at the rustic Aguanga Market.

After stocking up on water, proceed southeast on the Highway 79 shoulder. You'll arrive at the Oak Grove stage station after climbing for several miles.

The historic marker there commemorates the Butterfield Overland Mail, which linked San Francisco to the Midwest from 1858 to 1861. A little farther up the road, another sign marks where Camp Wright was established to guard the lines of communication in this area. As you make your weary way along the highway, it's diverting to imagine what this corner of the world looked like on horseback in 1858 instead of on wheels in the 1990s.

Sunshine Summit, at 35 miles, features a small store and a Mexican restaurant. The town's name seems doubly cheery when you realize that "summit" means that downhill awaits you just ahead. Your starting point lies a bit over two miles away. You've now covered 37 miles (40 miles with the side trips to High Point and the store at Aguanga).

Note: To shorten this trip, making it a fair bit easier, you can set up a car shuttle between the starting point near Warner Springs and the town of Aguanga.

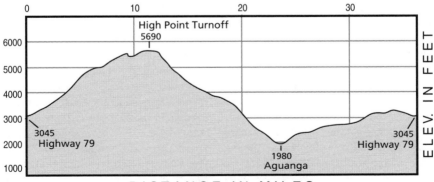

Trip 50. Indian Flats Loop

Starting Point: Warner Springs
GPS: Lat/Long 33° 17' 11", 116° 39' 34";
UTM 11S 531703mE 3682884mN
Distance: 25 miles
Elevation Gain: 2050 feet
Riding Time: 3 hours
Road Conditions: Graded and rough dirt
roads; paved highway with narrow
shoulder
Traffic Conditions: Light to moderate
Difficulty: ***
Equipment: Mountain bike

Where can you go to do some riding in the dirt after the rains come? Not on most of the county's backcountry dirt roads and trails, which turn slippery when wet. Instead, try this one. We route you over dirt roads cut into solid rock and decomposed granite soil. The runoff either drains away quickly or sinks into the porous, sand-like soil.

You begin at the Lost Valley Road turnoff (previously called Indian Flats Road) along Highway 79, 1.6 miles west of Warner Springs. The first few miles up Lost Valley Road are mostly paved (or rather expediently oiled), with alternating stretches of graded dirt road. You make your way uphill through low scrub at first, then through a more interesting mix of ribbonwood and manzanita chaparral. The road swings northeast and then north, and there's a view of Hot Springs Mountain (highest in San Diego County at 6533 feet) in the southeast. It's the one with the old fire lookout tower on top.

Just after 4 miles, a gated road intersects on the right. This leads to the Pacific Crest Trail (strictly off-limits to bicycles). You can see statuesque Coulter pines on the ridge above; but alas, you never get high enough on this ride to get close to them. Pines and other conifers tend to grow no lower than about 4000 feet in most of San Diego County.

The road becomes somewhat level, passing under the stony gaze of a boulder-stacked promontory to the east. At 6.3 miles, the main road veers left and dives down to Indian Flats Campground. A lesser road continues east; you'll return to this intersection after a stop at the campground.

The campground, which lies in a live-oak-shaded bowl, is open much of the year. You can fill up water bottles here and perhaps take off on foot (downhill) to the bubbling San Luis Rey River, about 400 yards away.

After climbing back to the intersection, continue northwest on the now-more-primitive Lost Valley Truck Trail. Stay right at the next fork 0.3 mile ahead. You descend slightly to where you must cross the willow- and sycamore-lined San Luis Rey River. This *is* a muddy spot during the rainy season. The water is sometimes high enough to engulf your bottom bracket—assuming you can get across without dismounting. You'll find a great spot for a rest or a picnic just downstream, where the stream cascades over polished rock slabs.

After the stream crossing, you ride uphill along an oak-shaded ravine, and then much more steeply up a chaparral-covered hillside to a 4368-foot summit. The view from there extends across miles of virtually untouched open space. The 6000+ foot heights of Bucksnort Mountain and Hot Springs Mountain are visible along the east horizon.

A mile of descent brings you to paved Chihuahua Valley Road and back to civilization. Hardly anyone in San Diego knows of the sparsely populated, quiet community of Chihuahua Valley, which is probably what the local inhabitants prefer.

After a left turn on Chihuahua Valley Road, a breezy descent takes you down to Highway 79. A modest climb of two miles south on the highway leads to Sunshine Summit. Then it's easy street as the remaining miles are effortlessly ticked away.

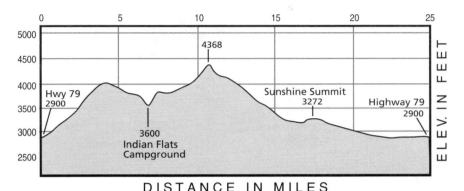

Trip 51. Santa Ysabel - Mesa Grande Tour

Starting Point: Santa Ysabel
GPS: Lat/Long 33° 6′ 34″, 116° 40′ 22″;
UTM 11S 530522mE 3663262mN
Distance: 22.5 miles
Elevation Gain: 1950 feet
Riding Time: 2.5 hours
Road Conditions: Smooth roads with narrow shoulders
Traffic Conditions: Light to moderate
Difficulty: ***
Equipment: Any multi-geared bike

The Indians called it *Took-uh-mack*, meaning "the place behind the ridge." Its official name, *Mesa Grande*, is Spanish for "large tableland." Together these two names imply, quite accurately, a kind of Shangri-La hidden from the view of most travelers.

At an elevation of over 3000 feet, this mountain plateau is more reminiscent of the rolling meadows and wooded slopes of central California's coast ranges than San Diego County's typical rock-ribbed

foothills. Through the heart of Mesa Grande runs a meandering country road. Newly widened and resurfaced, it serves only the light traffic generated by the handful of local residents. By any standard, it's surely one of the finest roads to cycle on in the county.

The tiny crossroads town of Santa Ysabel—well-known for its popular Dudley's Bakery—is a good starting point for our loop up Highway 79 and back along the meandering Mesa Grande Road. If you can get an early-morning start at Santa Ysabel, you'll find that traffic on fast, straight Highway 79 is practically nil.

Head north on Highway 79 out of town. After two miles, there's a climb of about one and one-half miles to a broad summit. An exhilarating downhill run follows, requiring neither pedaling

Mesa Grande Road

nor the use of the brakes. Lake Henshaw, and the Palomar Observatory's 200-inch telescope dome are visible straight ahead. During early morning, a blanket of fog often covers the lake.

At the bottom of the grade, turn left on Highway 76. After two more miles, go left at Mesa Grande Road. Only the strongest riders will remain on the pedals during the 1.5 miles that follow. Walking the bike can be pleasant enough, though, with large oaks providing intermittent shade. The expansive view often includes distant San Jacinto Peak, snow-capped in winter.

After topping out, Mesa Grande Road rolls generally southward over prime cattle-grazing country. At one point, it twists through a dense arboreal canopy. You'll cross some Indian reservation land and pass the defunct Mesa Grande store. On the slopes hereabouts are mines that have produced tourmaline, beryl, garnet, topaz, and other semiprecious gemstones.

More rolling, oak-dotted hills follow, ending with a steep downgrade that takes you back to Highway 79. Stop, if you wish, at the Santa Ysabel Mission, a nicely restored version of the original *asistencia*, or sub-mission of the San Diego mission established here in 1818. Visitors are welcome.

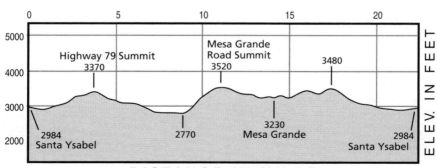

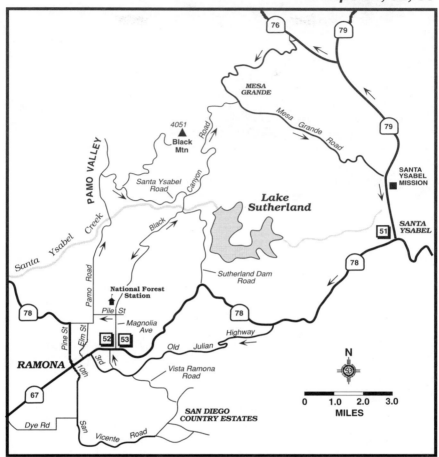

Trip 52. Black Canyon Tour

Starting Point: Ramona
GPS: Lat/Long 33° 3′ 4″, 116° 50′ 38″;
UTM 11S 514564mE 3656774mN
Distance: 37 miles
Elevation Gain: 2700 feet
Riding Time: 4 hours
Road Conditions: Smooth, paved roads with narrow to wide shoulders; smooth to rough dirt roads
Traffic Conditions: Light, except moderate to heavy on Highway 79
Difficulty: ***
Equipment: Mountain bike

Minutes north of Ramona lie several scenic canyons that offer splendid riding for those who care to venture off the main highway. Black Canyon is the best of these. When the winter rains come, runoff fills the bathtub-like rock pools in the bottom of the canyon. When the warm days of spring and summer come, the locals and others scramble down to visit them for a cool dip. Besides Black Canyon, the tour described here loops

Black Canyon Road

through the rolling hills of Mesa Grande and down the Old Julian Highway—a curvy, quiet country lane.

Begin at the intersection of Magnolia Avenue and Highway 78, just east of Ramona. You'll find roadside parking space nearby. Start by heading north on Magnolia Avenue. Magnolia turns into Black Canyon Road, passes the Cleveland National Forest Ranger Station, and continues through Valle De Los Amigos, a quiet valley with a few houses and scattered farmlands. The pavement soon ends and the road starts climbing into Cleveland National Forest land.

At 5.2 miles, you roll over a crest and begin a breezy, 2.2-mile downhill run. Oak- and sycamore-lined Santa Ysabel Creek lies to the left. At 7.4 miles, you cross an old bridge over Santa Ysabel Creek and begin a long, steady climb that will take you up along the east wall of Black Canyon—a tributary of Santa Ysabel Creek.

A locked gate on the left blocks the entrance (for cars) to the old Black Canyon Campground, which has been closed for many years now. At a point 0.6 mile after the bridge, a short, paved section of the road marks an area where people

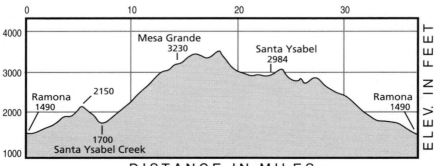

park their cars when visiting the creek below.

The next few miles of winding ascent are delightfully shaded at frequent intervals by wide-spreading live oaks. You'll briefly cross the Mesa Grande Indian Reservation and arrive at the paved Mesa Grande Road (14.0 miles). Turn right, pass the closed Mesa Grande Store and an old barn, and roll on through some of the finest rural scenery in the county. Spring-green or summer-golden, the oak-dotted, grassy hillsides of Mesa Grande are a throwback to California's rural past. A final, steep section of Mesa Grande Road takes you down to Highway 79.

Turn right and pedal past the Santa Ysabel Mission on your way to Santa Ysabel (22.6 miles). There you'll turn right and head west on Highway 78, but not before an obligatory stop at Dudley's Bakery. Early in the day you can get unsliced bread hot out of the oven. Just past the bottom of a long downgrade at 28.4 miles, turn left onto Old Julian Highway. This used to be the main route

to Julian, back in the days when roads were little more than reworked wagon tracks. Pasture land dotted with grazing horses and cows and an occasional windmill provide a nice backdrop. At 31.4 miles, there's a shady stretch good for a final rest stop.

At 35.3 miles, watch for Neighborly Lane on your left. Immediately afterward look for Amigos Road—an intersecting dirt road marked by rural mail boxes. Turn right, and right again at the next fork to return to Highway 78. Make a right and return to your starting point.

Options: To shorten the trip considerably, you can make use of Sutherland Dam Road. This road is rough dirt north of the lake and otherwise paved. For a 16-mile loop, use Black Canyon Road, Sutherland Dam Road, and Highway 78 (be careful of fast traffic down through the sharp curves on 78). For a 26-mile loop, starting at or near Lake Sutherland, use Sutherland Dam Road, Black Canyon Road, Mesa Grande Road, Highway 79, and Highway 78.

Trip 53. Pamo Valley Tour

Starting Point: Ramona
GPS: Lat/Long 33° 3′ 5″, 116° 50′ 38″; UTM 11S 514564mE 3656774mN
Distance: 20 miles
Elevation Gain: 1800 feet
Riding Time: 3 hours
Road Conditions: Smooth to rough dirt roads; smooth, paved roads with narrow to wide shoulders.
Traffic Conditions: Light
Difficulty: ***
Equipment: Mountain bike

Just north of Ramona lies the isolated, pristine Pamo Valley and a large slice of the Cleveland National Forest. This

ride takes you through the valley, up along dirt roads on the flank of Black Mountain, and past scenic Black Canyon. A panoramic view from Black Mountain's summit is yours to enjoy as well if you tackle a nearly 12-mile-long, optional side trip near the midpoint of the ride.

Start near the intersection of Magnolia Avenue and Highway 78, about 1 mile east of Ramona's town center. There's roadside parking nearby. Go north on Magnolia for 1.1 mile, then turn left on

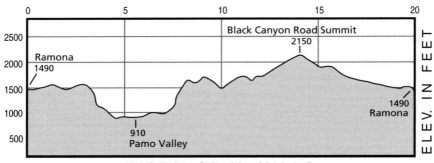

DISTANCE IN MILES

Pile Street. Go another 0.8 mile and turn right (north) on Pamo Road. Thankfully, the area ahead is still rural, with plenty of grazing horses and an occasional windmill. Pamo Road climbs a bit, then descends steeply toward oak-fringed Pamo Valley. On the way down, your gaze takes in the length and breadth of the valley. Santa Ysabel and Temescal creeks snake down the bottom, mostly hidden by thick bands of oaks and sycamores. A long-standing plan to flood this valley by constructing a huge dam at the lower end has, as of this writing, been sidetracked by adverse environmental impact reports.

Down in the bottom of the valley you'll cross Santa Ysabel Creek on a concrete bridge, and move on toward the oak-dotted flats where cattle graze. At 5.7 miles from the start, pavement gives way to a typical washboard dirt road. At 7.1 miles, turn right on the dirt road marked UPPER SANTA YSABEL (12S07).

The road immediately starts climbing and offers better and better views as you rise out of the valley. The hillsides are covered with mostly sage-scrub vegetation; if you're here in spring you'll see a great display of blooming yuccas. At the next junction (8.6 miles), bear right on what is signed SANTA YSABEL

ROAD (12S07). To the left is the route to Black Mountain—see Options below. The Santa Ysabel Road ahead may be closed to motorized traffic, but it's always open to hikers and bikers.

A short downhill stretch takes you across a small drainage densely shaded by oaks—this makes a good picnic spot near the midpoint of the ride. Then, for another three miles, you generally contour on the slopes above Santa Ysabel Creek, with many small ups and downs. During the rainy season, the oak- and sycamore-lined canyon bottom comes alive with the sounds of cascading water. Around 11 miles, the road elbows north to follow Black Canyon, and there's a gate that's easy to squeeze around if closed and locked. At 12.0 miles a short, downhill stretch brings you to a concrete stream crossing and the remains of Black Canyon Campground, which was closed many years ago. Follow the partially paved road to the right, up the hill and past another gate, to well-graded Black Canyon Road. Turn right there.

Just after you cross Santa Ysabel Creek on an old bridge, there's a rough road intersecting on the left. It leads to Lake Sutherland—a possible side trip. The San Diego Aqueduct, fed by the reservoir, follows the Santa Ysabel Creek canyon. The pipeline is visible here and there as you cruise along the road.

A winding, uphill stretch leads to a summit at 14.8 miles, where the Ramona valley comes into view ahead. The road slips downward into the agreeably named Valle de los Amigos, and becomes paved. You'll pass Goose Valley Ranger Station (which doubles as the Cleveland National Forest's Palomar District headquarters) on the right. Continue straight as Black Canyon Road becomes Magnolia Avenue, and return to the starting point.

Options: The side trip up Black Mountain Road (11S04) adds a round-trip distance of 12 miles and an elevation gain and loss of 2400 feet. Sturdy mountain bikes are absolutely required for this. The grade is mostly moderate throughout, but ranges from virtually flat to quite steep. You may have to walk your bike along one especially steep, rocky stretch about 4.5 miles up. There's not much shade on the way, but the 360-degree view from the top of Black Mountain gives a unique perspective of the mountains and foothills of San Diego County. Rather close at hand are Palomar Mountain in the north, the rolling hills of Mesa Grande to the east, and Lake Sutherland to the south. Some years ago, the ruins of an old fire lookout tower stood on Black Mountain's summit. Now, only the foundation is apparent.

Trip 54. Julian Tour

Starting Point: Julian
GPS: Lat/Long 33° 4' 42", 116° 36' 6"; UTM 11S 537172mE 3659843mN
Distance: 17 miles
Elevation Gain: 1850 feet
Riding Time: 2 hours
Road Conditions: Smooth roads with narrow shoulders
Traffic Conditions: Light to moderate
Difficulty: **
Equipment: Any multi-geared bike

Nestled in a landscape strongly reminiscent of northern California's Mother Lode region, the town of Julian is renowned as the center of an 1870s mini-Gold Rush. The town began in 1870 as a mining district under the chairmanship of Mike Julian, an ex-Confederate captain. The district was organized just after prospector Drury Baily's discovery of a gold-bearing quartz ledge nearby. In the first month of frantic activity, 260 claims and 40 noteworthy discoveries were made. Thousands of miners and would-be miners from San Diego and other southern California settlements flooded the new town site.

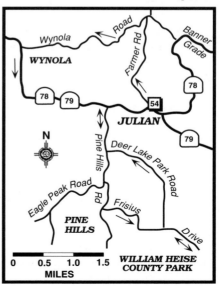

Trip 54

Farmer Road

Despite the mining bust a few years later, Julian never died. Its legacy in the early twentieth century had became that of apples, a crop well suited to the cool mountain climate. Nowadays the Julian-area economy thrives on apple growing, tourism, and real estate, especially the latter.

Several back roads around Julian offer superb cycling opportunities, provided you have a low set of gears to negotiate the occasional steep grades. A double-loop route is suggested here. If you ride the northern loop only, the distance is nine miles. The southern loop only, with the side trip to William Heise

County Park, is ten miles as measured from the start/end point at Julian.

An early start is recommended to avoid the tourists, who typically arrive in droves beginning about 10 a.m. Park anywhere in town, and begin by pedaling north on Main Street past the picturesque storefronts.

Once out of town, Main Street becomes Farmer Road. After passing through a scenic section of tawny or green (depending on the season) hills dotted with oaks and pines, you arrive at Wynola Road. Turn left and begin a gradual, twisting descent across an upland meadow, and then down through a narrow, deeply shaded canyon. You eventually arrive at Wynola, a crossroads settlement best known for its cluster of restaurants and fruit stands. Depending on the season, you could try a cup of hot or ice-cold apple cider, or a slice of Julian apple pie.

From Wynola, head south on Highway 78/79, mixing with what might be fairly heavy tourist traffic. A right turn at Pine Hills Road puts you once again onto a quiet byway. Wind through the shady community of Pine Hills, and then turn left at Frisius Road—toward Heise Park. To the south you'll spot the rounded summit of Cuyamaca Peak in nearby Cuyamaca Rancho State Park. Frisius Road takes you right down to the Heise Park entrance. For a small day-use fee, you can picnic beneath the spreading

oaks and explore on foot several interesting loop trails.

To return to Julian, go back on Frisius Road to Deer Lake Park Road and turn right. Near the summit ahead you'll probably notice some handsome specimens of manzanita, a rather common California shrub with smooth, reddish bark and dark red berries that resemble and taste like tiny apples. Manzanita fruits (*manzanita* is Spanish for "little apple") can be thought of as Julian's original apples.

Turn right at Pine Hills Road and right again on Highway 78/79. When you arrive back in Julian, take the time to play the role of tourist. Visit the Julian Museum and browse around the shops. Don't miss the old-fashioned soda fountain at the Julian Drug Store.

Trip 55. Cuyamaca Grand Tour

Starting Point: Cuyamaca Rancho State Park Distance: 18 miles
GPS: Lat/Long 32° 54' 32", 116° 34' 29"; UTM 11S 539772mE 3641089mN
Elevation Gain: 2000 feet
Riding Time: 4 hours
Road Conditions: Graded and rough dirt fire roads; smooth, paved highway with narrow shoulder.
Traffic Conditions: Moderate on highway; otherwise little or no traffic
Difficulty: ***
Equipment: Mountain bike

Cuyamaca Rancho State Park sprawls across roughly 45 square miles of upland San Diego County, a mere hour's drive from downtown San Diego. Near the park's western edge, Cuyamaca Peak stands at 6512 feet above sea level—the county's second highest point. The park is well known for its 100-mile trail system, which allow hikers, equestrians and, of late, mountain bikers to

explore its surprisingly attractive meadows and forests. The Indian name *Cuyamaca*, which means something like "the place where it rains," is suggestive of the local microclimate here. About 40 inches of precipitation arrives yearly—enough to sustain beautiful forests of oaks, pines, firs, and cedars.

Nearly half of the park is reserved as state wilderness, where policy prohibits the use of any vehicles including bicycles. On this consistently scenic and moderately challenging route, we direct you over old fire roads that steer clear of these prohibited areas. If you're interested in further exploration of the park, you can obtain from park headquarters or from any campground a map that indicates trails suitable for each kind of use—hiking, equestrian, and bicycling. Our map includes park roads (paved roads and fire roads) that are open to bicycles.

Start at the Sweetwater River bridge parking area at mile 4.8-4.9 on Highway 79 (just north of Green Valley Campground). Remember to display your National Forest Adventure Pass in your parked vehicle. Ride north a short distance, then turn across the highway (cautiously) when you spot the gated fire road on the left. Once on the fire road, you turn right almost immediately and continue north on Japacha Fire Road. You climb sometimes easily, sometimes moderately through pines and oaks. As you sidle up closer to trickling Japacha Creek, the forest becomes thicker and darker and there's a hint of dampness in the air. Near Japacha Spring, you'll cross the creek and continue climbing easily along the lower flank of Cuyamaca Peak.

At 2.1 miles, turn left on Fern Flat Fire Road and continue uphill. Stay right as lesser paths join from the left. When you reach the paved Lookout Road—"Cuyamaca Peak Fire Road" on most maps—jog right momentarily before resuming your northwest course along Cuyamaca Peak's flank. You're now working your way downhill, gently at first then more steeply, past Azalea Spring (water available here) and on to

a crossing of the graded Milk Ranch Road, (6.1 miles). Turn right on Milk Ranch Road and enjoy a nice, rather smooth spin down to Highway 79 at the former Boy Scout Camp entrance.

Turn right and follow the highway for 0.5 mile, then go left on the road to Stonewall Mine. One mile later, just short of the mine site itself, stay right, go around the gate and take the road to Los Vaqueros Group Horse Camp. After another 0.4 mile, turn left, off the pavement, onto Stonewall Creek Fire Road.

You're now crossing a beautiful, grassy swale with a vista of the three definitive summits of the Cuyamaca range—North Peak, Middle Peak, and Cuyamaca Peak. In about a mile, make a left on Soapstone Grade Fire Road. In the late spring, blooming lupine adorns an otherwise dry and rough stretch. After a bit, Soapstone Grade pitches downward, and you'll have to exercise a bit of bike-handling skill to make it safely to the bottom. It's not uncommon to pass riders walking their bikes up the hot, sun-exposed road.

Not much effort and skill is needed from now on. When you reach the foot of Soapstone Grade, turn right and coast easily along Upper Green Valley Fire

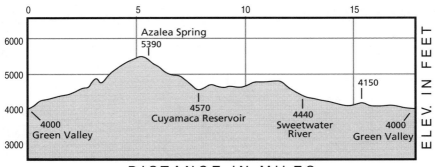

DISTANCE IN MILES

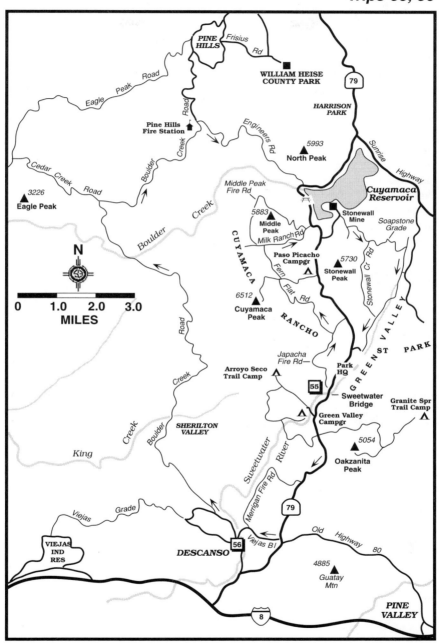

Road. You'll cross the trickling upper Sweetwater River several times and enjoy the benefit of overarching live oak trees. Stay left at the next junction, continue south on the wide gravel road, go through the gate into Camp Cuyamaca (school district camp), and skirt the camp and the park headquarters/museum to reach Highway 79. Turn left there and complete the easy return to your starting point at the Sweetwater River bridge.

Options: At the expense of about 4.5 extra miles and an extra 700 feet of elevation gain, you can loop around the north shoulder of Middle Peak.

Middle Peak's slopes have the largest coniferous trees in the park—sugar pines for the most part. You'll recognize them by their drooping branches, long cones, and amber-colored, puzzle-pattern bark. When you reach Milk Ranch Road at 6.1 miles, turn left, coast downhill, staying right at the next two intersections, and then start your climb up the switchbacking Middle Peak Fire Road.

You can also shorten our "grand tour" by about 1.5 miles by staying on Stonewall Creek Fire Road instead of using Soapstone Grade Fire Road to get to Upper Green Valley Fire Road.

Trip 56. Boulder Creek - Engineers Loop

Starting Point: Descanso
GPS: Lat/Long 32° 51' 12", 116° 36' 54"; UTM 11S 536029mE 3634907mN
Distance: 39.5 miles
Elevation Gain: 3200 feet
Riding Time: 6 hours
Road Conditions: Graded dirt roads; smooth, paved roads with narrow shoulders
Traffic Conditions: Light to moderate
Difficulty: ****
Equipment: Mountain bike

This ride is one of the longest mountain bike rides in this book. You'll get a taste of the raw, scrub-covered hills of the Cuyamaca foothills, and also pass through mixed forests and meadows quite reminiscent of the Sierra Nevada foothills. In the big picture, you'll be circumnavigating most of the Cuyamaca mountain range—about half on dirt road and the rest on pavement.

A good starting point is the town of Descanso, quickly reached from Interstate 8, some 35 miles east of San Diego. Exit I-8 at the Cuyamaca/Highway

79 offramp, go 1.3 miles north, and turn left at the Descanso junction. Go another mile and park near Perkins Store. This store was established in 1875, and is a great place to get a cold drink after the ride.

You can do the ride in either direction, but we'd suggest going clockwise—uphill on the rough sections of Boulder Creek Road and downhill on the paved highway. Start off with plenty of water; there's no drinking water for the first 20 mostly uphill miles. Also, leave early (unless it's winter) to avoid the intense midday heat.

Begin by riding north on Oak Grove Drive. A gradual climb takes you past horse corrals and pastures. When you reach the first crest, turn right on Boulder Creek Road. As you start a rapid descent, with a cool wind in your face, look up to see Cuyamaca Peak in the distance. You'll have plenty of opportunity to view it from all sides in the next several hours.

Cattle chute, Boulder Creek Road

At the bottom of the grade, at 5.0 miles, you'll cross King Creek on a concrete ford. The road begins climbing here. At 6.5 miles, the pavement ends and the graded road begins. The view west toward the Capitan Grande Indian Reservation and Eagle Peak are very nice. Sage and manzanita cover the hillsides in this area. Occasional clusters of oaks offer shade where various ravines intersect the road.

After a while you reach a 3934-foot summit, only two miles southwest of Cuyamaca Peak that rises some 2600 feet higher. The road then goes down again until you cross Boulder Creek on a concrete ford at 12.1 miles. Most of Boulder Creek's upstream drainage comes from Cuyamaca Reservoir; its flow often depends on the amount of water released from there. A couple of miles downstream, there is a triple set of

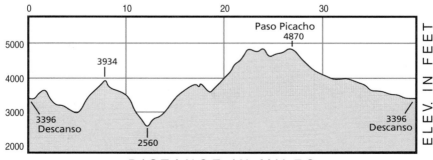

waterfalls, the "Three Sisters," in a deep canyon occasionally visited by hikers. Also nearby is the Devils Punchbowl, a circular feature worn in the bed of Boulder Creek, located on private property.

You climb again, up past the junction of Cedar Creek Road, and ultimately into a sparse forest of oak and pine trees. Middle Peak, crowned with forests of oak, incense-cedar, white fir, and several varieties of pine, is now visible to the east. After about two more miles you reach the junction of Engineers Road. The Pine Hills Fire Station is here with water, if needed. This is a popular starting place for mountain bikers who travel a tough, 21-mile loop to the west and south consisting of Eagle Peak Road, Cedar Creek Road, and Boulder Creek Road.

On our trip, you'll make a right on Engineers Road. There's more climbing through oaks and conifers. At 22.7 miles, you reach the boundary of Cuyamaca Rancho State Park. Incense cedar and oaks complement each other as you continue winding up a moderately steep hill. On several of the turns you'll have a great view south and east toward tree-covered Middle Peak and chaparral-covered Stonewall Peak.

After topping out at a rather indistinct crest, you will enjoy a gently curving, mostly downhill ride toward Cuyamaca Reservoir. Turn right when you reach Highway 79 and ride around the shoreline to the store and picnic area on the left—a good spot for a refreshment break.

Beyond the lake, there's a moderate climb on the highway up to Paso Picacho Campground (28.0 miles)—the highest point of the whole ride at 4870 feet. You've paid your dues to gravity now. The mostly downhill run ahead starts with a fast stretch that includes a couple of very sharp curves. Watch your speed! You'll fly by the Park Headquarters/Indian Museum entrance, glide through the meadows alongside the Sweetwater River, and climb a bit to a summit just beyond Green Valley Campground. A further descent down tight and then easy turns takes you to Viejas Boulevard (37.2 miles)—the turnoff you'll take to go directly back to Descanso. A country store/fruit stand sits next to this intersection.

Several interesting houses, including one made of stone called Rock Haven, divert your attention as you complete the home stretch in Descanso Valley. That cold drink at the Perkins Store will taste mighty good when you finally arrive.

Trip 57. Cuyamaca - Laguna Triangle

Starting Point: Pine Valley
GPS: Lat/Long 32° 49′ 17″, 116° 31′ 41″;
UTM 11S 544165mE 3631400mN
Distance: 44 miles
Elevation Gain: 4050 feet
Riding Time: 5 hours
Road Conditions: Smooth roads with mostly narrow shoulders
Traffic Conditions: Light to moderate; heavy on weekends on Highway 79
Difficulty: ****
Equipment: Any multi-geared bike

Forty to fifty miles east of San Diego, the crest of the Peninsular Ranges forms a great barrier separating the foothills and coastal plain to the west from the inland deserts to the east. Here, the tops of the Cuyamaca and Laguna mountains rise to elevations in excess of 6000 feet. These mountains wring out moisture delivered to San Diego County by winter storm systems from the northwest and, to a lesser extent, by subtropical summer storms from Mexico.

Since the annual precipitation in this area can be as much as 50 inches, beautiful growths of coniferous trees are found here and there. First-time visitors to the area are often surprised to find such a lush, shady environment so far south in California. Even more startling is the spectacular, steep drop from these forested heights to the parched desert to the east. This mountain-desert contrast is seen well along parts of Sunrise Highway in the Laguna Mountains.

While this "triangle" tour of the Cuyamacas and Lagunas is arguably the most scenic bike route in San Diego County, it's important to be aware that tourists in cars love the area too. If you can swing it, the weekdays are best for touring. On most weekends, Highway 79 and the south half of Sunrise Highway

are too busy for carefree cycling. An early start, though, can mitigate this.

Pine Valley, conveniently located off Interstate 8 about 40 miles east of San Diego, is a good starting point. Our roughly triangular-shaped loop route can be done in either direction, though clockwise seems to take better advantage of normal wind patterns.

Head west on Old Highway 80 down to the bridge over Pine Valley Creek. Next comes a steep climb to Guatay Summit and the tiny town of Guatay. It was a busy roadside stop before the completion of Interstate 8 in the early 1970s. A nice downhill run through oaks and pastureland follows.

Look up on the slopes of Guatay Mountain to the south and you will spot some dark clumps of vegetation rising above the chaparral. They are Tecate cypress, indigenous only to a few isolated mountain locations in Orange County, San Diego County and Baja California.

Turn right at Highway 79, and make your way gradually uphill over several miles of roadway intermittently shaded by oaks. In a few miles, a sign announces your entry into Cuyamaca Rancho State Park. You continue past Green Valley Campground, up through the grassy swales of Green Valley, past the turnoff for park headquarters and the Indian Museum, and up along the delightfully shaded bed of a trickling brook called Cold Stream.

A little higher, the pointed, alabaster summit of Stonewall Peak comes into clear view on the right. At Paso Picacho Campground, the road tops out and begins a moderate descent toward Cuyamaca Reservoir. Set amid oaks, pines and cedars, the campground includes a pleasant picnic area close to the highway. At the very least, a stop here is worthwhile to fill up water bottles.

The resort/picnic area on the west side of Cuyamaca Reservoir offers an opportunity for a sit-down meal. Food and water are not available again on the route until you reach Mount Laguna, 16 mostly-uphill miles away.

Beyond the resort area, Highway 79 curves around the reservoir dam and continues through gently rolling meadows along the shoreline. During wet years, the shallow northern flood plain of the reservoir fills to capacity; at other times cattle graze the marshy or grassy bottom. During April and May the roadside wildflowers in this area can be really eye-popping.

Turn right at Sunrise Highway and go up and over a small summit followed by a mile-long flat stretch of road. Then settle in for many miles of moderate climbing relieved occasionally by brief level or downhill stretches. The road follows the crest of the Laguna Mountains southeast, sometimes chiseling along its rocky eastern escarpment. For a few miles it passes through a small part of Anza-Borrego Desert State Park, the

nearly 1000-square-mile park that occupies most of what you can see to the east. Although it's tempting to peer over the edge at the desert below, be wary of fast cars and sudden crosswind gusts.

After you pass Pioneer Mail Picnic Area, there's plenty of shade. Nearly pure stands of Jeffrey pine, with black oaks mixed in here and there, give these higher parts of the Laguna Mountains a well-ordered, park-like appearance.

The long upgrade ends at the turnoff for Desert View Picnic Area, just short of the small village of Mount Laguna. You can get a better view of the desert by going a quarter mile up the access road (just north of the picnic area access road) leading to the old Air Force radar station on Stephenson Peak. Mount Laguna village includes a general store, restaurant, and Forest-Service information center.

Beyond Mount Laguna, Sunrise Highway rises a bit to attain the highest summit yet, then drops steadily for the next seven miles leading to Interstate 8. Just before the I-8 ramps, turn right on Old Highway 80 and coast down a final mile into Pine Valley. Enjoy the exhilarating trip down the mountain—you've earned it!

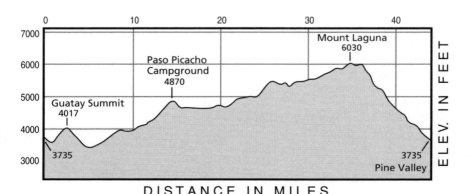

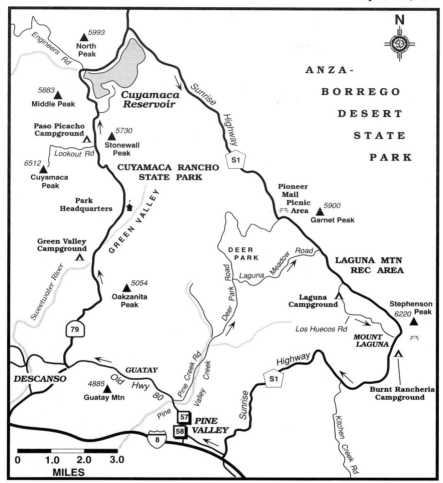

Trip 58. Noble Canyon Tour

Starting Point: Pine Valley
GPS: Lat/Long 32° 49' 17", 116° 31' 41";
UTM 11S 544165mE 3631400mN
Distance: 26.5 miles
Elevation Gain: 2950 feet
Riding Time: 5 hours
Road Conditions: Smooth to rough fire
roads; smooth, paved highway with
narrow shoulder
Traffic Conditions: Light to moderate
Difficulty: ****
Equipment: Mountain bike

This mountain bike ride has it all: steep climbs, exhilarating downhills, and the opportunity to ride through oak and pine forests. It also features some nice vistas of much of San Diego County's higher ground—the Cuyamaca and Laguna mountains.

The best starting point is the center of Pine Valley, right off Interstate 8 about 40 miles east of San Diego. You can ride the loop in either direction, but clockwise is better if you'd rather spend time going uphill on dirt and later enjoy a fast descent on pavement on the return leg.

Start by riding northwest on Old Highway 80, downhill to the old concrete bridge over Pine Valley Creek. After crossing the bridge, make a sharp right onto Pine Valley Road. The climbing is almost imperceptible at first as you work your way up the broad flood plain of the creek. After a few minutes you'll pass the trailhead for the Noble Canyon Trail and a picnic ground. Just ahead the road fords Pine Valley Creek and turns to dirt.

The area ahead is dotted with oaks and pines and a fair number of cabins on land leased from the Forest Service. Ignore the side roads; just keep going straight on the main road, which continues to parallel Pine Valley Creek. After the second stream crossing, you start an uphill pitch and soon reach a road fork. Bear right on the unsigned Deer Park Road, which continues to take you away from the Pine Valley Creek drainage. A short, brutal climb on rough, rocky road is just ahead.

The steep climb is soon over, and you descend just a bit before starting to follow a dry streambed moderately uphill. A few live oak trees cluster along the ravine bottom, providing some cool shade if you want it. At 5.4 miles, note the two water tanks on your right. Tragedy Springs, near this spot, flows into the tanks. There are an old abandoned shack and ruins nearby, perhaps the site of the tragedy—the murder of a child—that took place here in the 1950s.

Ahead, the road becomes paved for a while, but not without assuming a "stand-on-the-pedals" gradient. A large oak tree marks the end of the paved stretch, and the steepest part of the whole ride. Cross a cattle guard on the saddle just ahead, and turn right on Laguna Meadow Road (signed 14S05). Another steep, rocky section follows, taking you up to a ridge with views toward Noble Canyon and Pine Valley in the south, and north into Indian Creek canyon and the northern summits of the Laguna Mountains. At mile 7.4, a short spur road leads south to a ridgetop offering a 360-degree vista of the Cuyamacas and Lagunas. Take this little diversion if you want to relax and have a snack at a scenic spot.

Back on the main Laguna Meadow Road, there's a bit more climbing and then a descent to a T-intersection. Bear

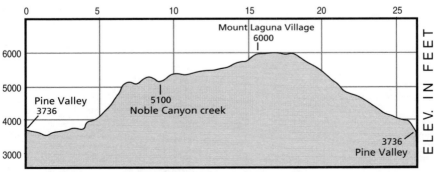

Jeffrey pine forest, Laguna Mountains

right and continue east into the upper reaches of Noble Canyon, which is abundantly clothed with stately Jeffrey pines and black oaks. You swing north along Noble Canyon's creek, and after some further climbing, cross over another cattle guard. Turn left at the next junction. You'll soon connect with pavement at a spot just south of a large meadow called Filaree Flat. This road takes you swiftly to Sunrise Highway, where you turn right (southeast).

After riding the highway for about 2 miles, turn right at the well-marked entrance to Laguna Campground. The campground has the first potable water on the route. Go straight past the outdoor amphitheater on the left to an apparent dead end. Ride on past the vehicle barrier and continue on pavement, which soon becomes dirt—this is Los Huecos Road. The next 2.5 miles of moderate uphills and lesser downhills are delightful. Beautiful oaks and pines surround you, and the wildflowers are really colorful during the first warm weeks after a wet winter. You'll pass more private cabins on leased national forest land.

When you reach Sunrise Highway (the highest elevation of the trip), you can get water at the Visitor's Information Office, just left. Immediately to the right is a country store and restaurant in the heart of the little village of Mount Laguna.

Your return to Pine Valley from the Laguna Mountains is by way of Sunrise Highway and a short, fast section of Old Highway 80 that parallels Interstate 8.

It's downhill almost the entire way, a loss of 2200 feet. Prevailing headwinds will likely slow your descent somewhat, limiting your freewheeling speed to no more than about 25 mph.

If there's still a bit of "off-road" adventure in you on the way down, then you can try your luck for a while on an older segment of Sunrise Highway. It splits from the newer highway a little below the lower end of Crouch Valley—the large meadow about half way down the mountain. Look for the gated road with the sign FIRE ROAD, DO NOT BLOCK. The rough old road meanders along the bottom of dry Scove Canyon for about 2.5 miles, and rejoins the new road at a large turnout 2 miles up from Interstate 8.

Trip 59. Lawson and Gaskill Peaks

Starting Point: East of Jamul
GPS: Lat/Long 32° 42′ 48″, 116° 42′ 18″; UTM 11S 527648mE 3619363mN
Distance: 13.5 miles
Elevation Gain: 1950 feet
Riding Time: 2 hours
Road Conditions: Rough dirt roads; paved roads with narrow shoulders
Traffic Conditions: Light
Difficulty: ***
Equipment: Mountain bikes only

Lawson and Gaskill peaks are two rock-ribbed bumps along a lofty ridge visible from many parts of San Diego. The bare bones of the earth are exposed on both: massive boulders lie heaped up like the result of some geologic catastrophe. Actually, the boulder heaps were caused by typical weathering and erosion of granitic rock. Here and in much of San Diego County, the bedrock is being slowly uplifted. The agents of

erosion—groundwater, rain, and even wind—have carved the rock into interesting forms, large and small.

A seldom-traveled dirt road passes near the summit of both peaks, allowing convenient access to either or both them—if you're willing to ditch your bike and scramble on foot. The view from the top of both peaks is splendid on a clear day, and there are lots of little hollows and crevices to explore in the fissured rock.

You begin along Lyons Valley Road, 11 miles east of Jamul. Park in either of two turnouts exactly at mile marker 13.0. Remember to display your National Forest Adventure Pass in your parked vehicle.

You'll expend most of your effort on this ride during the first two miles with a rather brutal climb of 1200 feet on the rough, rutty Carveacre Road. The road is open to vehicles, but not many seem to accept the challenge and risk. At the first road summit, Lawson Peak comes into view, and you can see how a straightforward scramble would lead to its boulder-crowned top.

After a small descent, turn right at the first intersection. Continue gradually descending for a short mile. Another, rather modest, climb begins as you work your way along the east shoulder of Gaskill Peak. Hikers have worn in a couple of hard-to-find trails leading through the chaparral to Gaskill's top. Even on the road, though, the view is impressive—especially to the east, where the corrugated landscape of chaparral and gleaming rock stretches for miles.

A fast descent takes you north into a flatter area dotted with rustic houses. You make your way downhill through a maze of roads, finally reaching pavement a short distance before reaching Japatul Road.

Turn right on Japatul Road, climb uphill for a mile, and turn right on Lyons Valley Road. The last few, mostly downhill miles on lonely Lyons Valley Road are a fitting climax for a great ride.

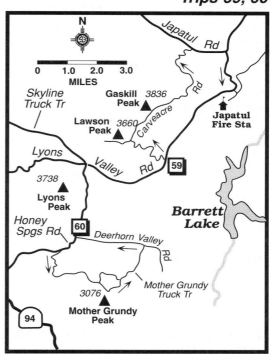

Trips 59, 60

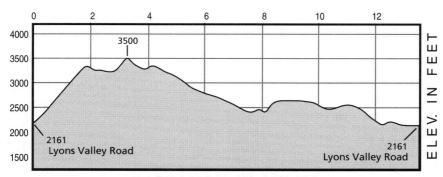

Trip 60. Mother Grundy Tour

Starting Point: East of Jamul
GPS: Lat/Long 32° 40′ 44″, 116° 45′ 8″;
UTM 11S 523236mE 3615532mN
Distance: 8 miles
Elevation Gain: 1250 feet
Riding Time: 1.25 hours
Road Conditions: Graded dirt road;
paved roads with narrow shoulders
Traffic Conditions: Light
Difficulty: **
Equipment: Mountain bike

To the old-timers of Jamul and Dulzura, the rocky profile of one nearby peak seemed to suggest the face of a woman of considerable presence (*Madre Grande*). The folksy-sounding "Mother Grundy"—the official name on contemporary maps—seems to be a Spanglish corruption of the original name.

This brief little ride takes you up past Mother Grundy Peak, and down into Deerhorn Valley—another of San Diego County's secluded rural communities.

Start at the intersection of Deerhorn Valley Road and Honey Springs Road. You can get there from Jamul by taking either Highway 94 to Honey Springs Road, or Skyline Truck Trail to Honey Springs Road. Find a place to park off the pavement on the shoulder of Deerhorn Valley Road.

Begin with a fast coast down Honey Springs Road. At 0.8 mile, don't miss the turn for Mother Grundy Truck Trail (a.k.a. Mother Grundy Road) on the left. This graded dirt road rises steadily through chaparral vegetation punctuated with granodiorite boulder flakes that look like shark teeth. The view to the west, toward Otay Lakes and the South Bay area, broadens as you climb.

You reach a summit at about 3 miles (from the start), and then descend east into a beautiful little oak-dotted basin. A private wild animal preserve sprawls on the right. Via Pamela, another dirt road, intersects on the left—it returns to Mother Grundy Truck Trail about a mile ahead. Mother Grundy Peak (on private property) rises behind it. At the east end of the basin, stay left and begin another, lesser climb, heading north.

After Via Pamela comes in from the left again, stay left at the next intersection just ahead. Continue on what seems to be the main road. You'll navigate through a maze of dirt splinter roads and driveways. When you finally reach the paved Deerhorn Valley Road, turn left and enjoy a speedy descent back to the starting point.

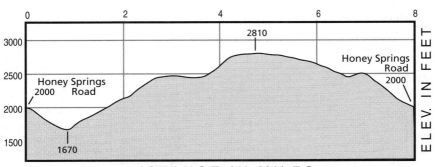

DISTANCE IN MILES

Trip 61. Los Pinos Tour

Starting Point: Near Lake Morena
GPS: Lat/Long 32° 43' 0", 116° 29' 57";
UTM 11S 546934mE 3619783mN
Distance: 16.7 miles
Elevation Gain: 1800 feet
Riding Time: 2.5 hours
Road Conditions: Poor dirt roads; narrow paved road
Traffic Conditions: Light
Difficulty: ***
Equipment: Mountain bikes only

Los Pinos Mountain's 4805-foot height hardly places it in the same league as the higher peaks of the Cuyamacas and Lagunas, but it *is* recognized for its fire lookout tower—one of only three remaining active lookouts in San Diego County. To get the best views, try this looping tour to the top of the mountain on a clear, cool late fall or winter day. Or, for a quick getaway in summer, come out very early in the morning or in late afternoon to escape the heat. From late July through mid-September, thunderheads often roll in during the afternoons, sometimes delivering a burst of rain. The clouds usually dissipate by late afternoon, leaving a glistening landscape redolent with the smell of wet earth and sage.

We suggest you start at the intersection of Corral Canyon Road and Buckman Springs Road (3.3 miles south of Interstate 8), so as to start with a good warm-up on the first few, rather flat miles of Corral Canyon Road. The road leads to the Corral Canyon Off-Road Vehicle Area. If you're riding on the weekend, watch out for cars and trucks hauling ORV machines on the narrow pavement. Be sure to display your National Forest Adventure Pass in your parked vehicle.

At a point 4.8 miles from the start, Corral Canyon Road bends sharply left and begins curving up a hillside. (You'll return to this point after you come down from the mountain.) Exactly at the bend, you'll see a locked gate on the right. This keeps out ORVs, but non-motorized travelers are allowed go though (probably the biggest challenge on this ride is getting your bike past this gate).

You continue riding uphill in the shade of live oaks, now on a dirt surface. After 0.5 mile, veer left on the Espinosa Trail. After another mile uphill through chaparral, you'll reach a saddle where Los Pinos Road intersects. Espinosa Trail continues west—eventually into the Pine Creek Wilderness, which is off-limits to bikes. You make a left turn on the road.

Steep and rocky in places, Los Pinos Road curves up along the north flank of Los Pinos Mountain, which is finally beginning to sport a decent growth of young Coulter pines. The 1970 Laguna fire burned across these slopes, destroying the much thicker pine forest that used to exist here. The mountain was named after *los pinos*—the pines.

Stay left where the spur road to Spur Meadow takes off. At the next intersection, higher still, another (gated) spur road slants left and continues curving up to the fire lookout tower on top. The extra climb is well worth the view. If you run into the fire spotter on duty (summer and fall), remember that he or she may be too busy to chat with you.

You can now look forward to lots of downhill riding. Return to Los Pinos Road, where you make a sharp left. After zigzagging down the south side of the

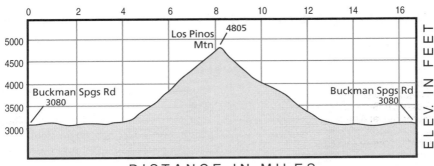

mountain, you arrive at a large clearing called Four Corners. Take the paved road on the left (Corral Canyon Road), curl down the slope (being cautious on the sharp curves), and return to point where you left the pavement earlier. Continue back to Buckman Springs Road the way you came.

Options: The Corral Canyon Off-Road Vehicle Area attracts a fair to large number of ORVers on weekends and holidays, but almost no one uses the area on weekdays. Motorcycle trails abound, so if you're into "single track" riding, this is a great place to go, as long as you don't have to share it with noisy machines.

Trip 61

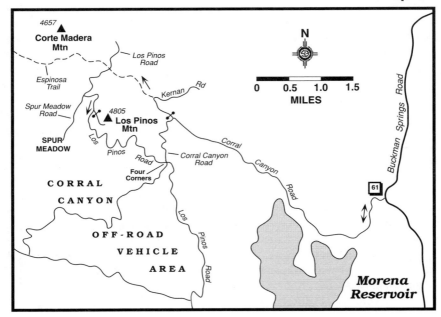

Trip 62. Campo - Boulevard Loop

Starting Point: Buckman Springs Rest Area (near Pine Valley)
GPS: Lat/Long 32° 45′ 34″, 116° 29′ 12″; UTM 11S 548081mE 3624559mN
Distance: 39 miles
Elevation Gain: 2650 feet
Riding Time: 4 hours
Road Conditions: Smooth roads with mostly narrow shoulders
Traffic Conditions: Light to moderate
Difficulty: ***
Equipment: All multi-geared bikes

Amid the rolling hills and gentle valleys of south San Diego County, you can get a glimpse of rural southern California, circa 1950. The topography of this border-hugging rural area is quite similar to that of north San Diego County's foothill areas, but the scenery and ambience differ completely. While most of North County's rural area is covered by orderly groves of citrus and avocado and dotted with modern ranch houses, here you find a picturesque mix of scrubby hillsides, rustic cattle ranches, natural oak groves, and tidy old-fashioned towns like Campo and Boulevard. Signs of wealth and prosperity are not particularly abundant: here and there along the highways are quite a number of old trailers with the usual wrecked autos out front.

A good place to park and begin this trip is anywhere *outside* the big rest area in the median of Interstate 8 at Buckman Springs Road, east of Pine Valley. (Technically you're not allowed to leave your car unaccompanied inside any California freeway rest area.) Remember to display your National Forest Adventure Pass in your parked vehicle.

Head south on Buckman Springs Road. For the next three miles you'll skirt the west edge of Cottonwood Valley. The valley is dotted with sturdy live oaks and also many cottonwood trees, distinguished by their textured grey trunks, pale limbs, and (in spring and summer) shimmering green leaves. During winter the denuded branches of the cottonwoods appear striking and ghostly.

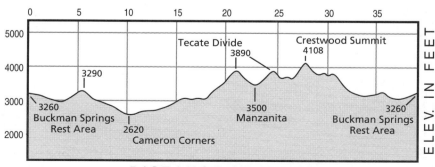

DISTANCE IN MILES

After crossing Cottonwood Creek on a narrow bridge and then climbing moderately for about two miles, you come to a **Y**-intersection on the right. This is Oak Drive, which leads into Morena Village and the county park and campground at Morena Reservoir (an interesting optional side trip). Within the island of this intersection, a plaque commemorates the unfortunate Charles M. Hatfield, the legendary rainmaker whose endeavors to bring rain to a parched San Diego County in 1916 were disastrously successful.

Ahead there's a flat stretch, then a nice downgrade to Highway 94 at Cameron Corners. Here you'll find a couple of cafes and a few other small businesses serving the Campo area. The center of Campo, with its historic old stone store and its new railroad museum, is 1.5 miles south of here by way of Highway 94. This offers another worthwhile digression at the expense of a little extra distance.

Our route continues east on Highway 94 past an old mill where feldspar used in the manufacture of porcelain bathroom fixtures was once processed. The next 12 miles are uphill, following the course of Campo Creek. At one point the highway passes under an enormous steel trestle. This is the "High Bridge" on the San Diego & Arizona Eastern railroad line. Not much rail traffic has passed this way since 1976, when Hurricane Kathleen severely damaged the line farther east in Carrizo Gorge.

Just before the next summit—Tecate Divide—the road leaves the shady bank of Campo Creek and climbs onto a gently rolling, but desolate tableland. Until recently, a fair number of wind turbines dotted these gentle hillsides, a testament to the strong and steady winds that make this one of southern California's better

Trip 62

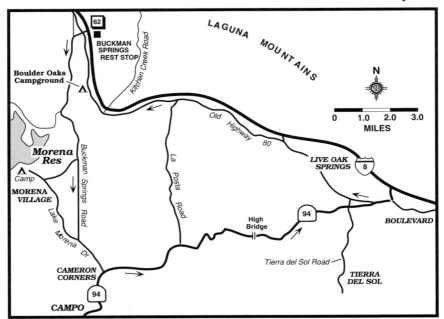

Old gas pumps, Live Oak Springs

areas for the production of wind-generated electricity. Unfortunately, most of the wind-power installations here did not survive because of economic reasons.

Beyond Tecate Summit, a fast downgrade leads to the side-by-side towns of Boulevard and Manzanita. Highway 94 turns north to join Interstate 8. Just east, on Old Highway 80, is the Wisteria Candy Cottage, famous for its Wisteria chocolate, founded in 1929. A nearby restaurant and a small store can provide snacks and drinks on a warm day. What may be this area's best claim to fame, however, is a widely circulated bumper sticker reading "Where The Hell Is Boulevard."

From Boulevard, go back toward the west, but this time on Old Highway 80. After crossing Tecate Divide again, you descend toward Live Oak Springs—an oak-shaded resort/camping area just off the highway. A 1.5-mile upgrade follows, passing by the new Golden Acorn Casino on your right. Just before the junction with Interstate 8, turn left (staying on Old Highway 80). Enjoy the final nine mostly downhill miles on this quiet frontage road, relieved of its former heavy traffic by the newer Interstate 8.

Trip 63. Around Granite Mountain

Starting Point: Near Scissors Crossing, Anza-Borrego Desert
GPS: Lat/Long 33° 3′ 41″, 116° 25′ 30″; UTM 11S 553687mE 3658054mN
Distance: 24 miles
Elevation Gain: 1950 feet
Riding Time: 4.5 hours
Road Conditions: Smooth, paved roads with narrow shoulders; unpaved roads ranging from smooth and sandy to very rough
Traffic Conditions: Light; moderate on Highway 78
Difficulty: ***
Equipment: Mountain bike

Trip 63

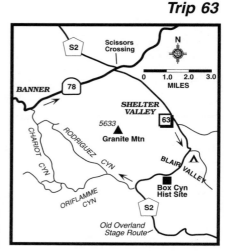

People who visit the vast and seemingly static Anza-Borrego Desert region are sometimes lulled into thinking that very little activity actually takes place in the desert. On this ride you'll discover that ain't necessarily so. As you ride along parts of the historic Southern Emigrant Trail and the route of the Butterfield Overland Mail, it's easy to visualize the plumes of dust kicked up by horses and wagons over a century ago. With another exercise of imagination, you might visualize the slow creeping—in fits and starts—of entire mountains over geologic time scales. The Elsinore, Earthquake Valley, and Chariot Canyon faults all run through this area.

To reach the starting point take Highway 78 from Julian down the Banner Grade, which leads east into the desert. (On the way down the grade, watch for signs of the Elsinore Fault etched low on the canyon wall to your left. Also notice the dirt road leading up a canyon to the right of the white, rock-lined letter **B** on the hill ahead of you. That is where you will be emerging on your bike during the ride.) At the Scissors Crossing junction, bear right on Highway S2,

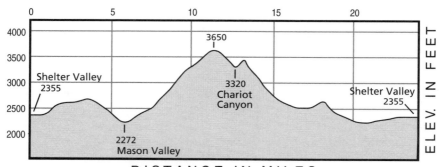

and continue about 4 miles to the country store at mile marker 21. This is a good starting point for the ride, and a convenient place to pick up refreshments. Be sure you set off with plenty of water or other liquids.

Begin by cycling south on S2 through Earthquake Valley—or, as the locals prefer, Shelter Valley. The low Pinyon Mountains are on your left and the monolithic Granite Mountain on your right. Soon you will have to push your pedals a bit to traverse the little pass separating Earthquake Valley from Blair Valley. A short distance east of this pass is Foot and Walker Pass, where passengers on the Butterfield Overland Mail in the 1850s often had to get out and help the driver push their wagon over the pass. The scattered vegetation in the area is characteristic of the high desert: creosote bush, ocotillo, cholla cactus, yucca and especially agave—the latter in spectacular bloom in springtime if the rains have been abundant.

The highway soon starts heading downhill into Box Canyon. A historical marker calls attention to a little gorge on the left where the Mormon Batallion cut a passage through a rocky defile to open the first wagon route into southern California. The route of the Southern Emigrant Trail and the Butterfield Overland Mail closely parallels the road in this area.

After the swift descent into broad Mason Valley, turn right at 5.7 miles onto the unpaved road marked with mailboxes and a sign for Oriflamme Canyon. Stay right at the **Y** in the road and follow the sandy streambed, which is filled with large desert willow shrubs—very aromatic in the late spring. It gets rougher ahead as the road veers in and out of the dry streambed. There are a few small

dwellings visible to the south, but soon you will leave them far behind. At 7.7 miles you pass through a gated fence. The road begins to climb toward the broad mouth of Oriflamme Canyon.

At the next junction, bear right on the signed road through Rodriguez Canyon, accompanied by a small powerline. (The road to the left continues through Oriflamme Canyon.) You're now riding parallel to the Elsinore Fault, one of the major splinter faults of the great San Andreas Fault, which lies well to the northeast. You'll cross the Rodriguez Canyon streambed several times in the next couple of miles. If the sand is dry, you can increase your traction by softening your tires a bit. Then, several steep, rocky slopes will force even the best riders to do some walking. Just past the second state park boundary sign, an abandoned cinder block building will be on your right. As you continue, look for the base of an overturned windmill almost hidden in the bushes to the left.

As you approach the head of the canyon, the landscape opens a bit, yielding to grass and scrub-oak vegetation. Granite Mountain looms majestically on your right. At 11.6 miles, you cross a cattle guard at the road summit. This is the highest point of the ride and affords a spectacular view north toward the smooth and barren San Felipe Valley and the rounded summits of the Volcan Mountains. Most of the small side roads you see in this area are access roads to old mines. Please respect all claims. Some are actively being worked for recovery of gold, and their owners have been known to aggressively defend these properties against anyone malicious or simply curious.

On the downslope ahead the road becomes wider and better maintained.

After several turns there are even better views into San Felipe Valley and also northwest straight up Banner Canyon. The obvious linear structure of Banner Canyon is due to horizontal movement along the Elsinore Fault.

At the next junction, stay left and pass alongside a beautiful green pasture with grazing cows and a backdrop of several mines, complete with tailing piles and headframes. At 12.9 miles, the road starts climbing again. You cross a ridge and then descend into the next drainage leading toward Chariot Canyon. Stay right at the next intersection and begin a fast downhill to the highway and the Banner

Store. The letter **B** that you spotted earlier in your car is on the hillside to the right as you approach the highway.

At the Banner Store you can fill your water bottle or grab a cold drink before zooming down the rest of Banner Grade to the desert below. The last few miles on pavement are generally downhill—punctuated by one small upgrade—and there's usually a strong tailwind. Don't miss the turn onto Highway S2 at Scissors Crossing. The intersection of Saddle Sore Lane, on the right, may be meaningful as you approach your starting point—the country store in Shelter Valley.

Trip 64. Borrego Valley Desert Ride

Starting Point: Borrego Springs
GPS: Lat/Long 33° 15′ 23″, 116° 22′ 27″;
UTM 11S 558299mE 3679694mN
Distance: 16.5 miles
Elevation Gain: 150 feet
Riding Time: 80 minutes
Road Conditions: Smooth roads with mostly wide shoulders
Traffic Conditions: Light to moderate
Difficulty: **
Equipment: Any bicycle

Borrego Valley has blue skies, warm temperatures, palm trees, a colorful backdrop of rugged mountains—and in the late winter and early spring, carpet-like expanses of wildflowers. It also has a good network of flat, paved roads that are perfect for touring on a bicycle. Bike racers from all over the country come here to train and to participate in U.S. Cycling Federation time trials and races. Casual cyclists often show up during the wildflower season to admire the scenery.

A good starting point for our easy-going Borrego Valley ride is Christmas

Circle, a traffic circle enclosing a small grassy park in the center of Borrego Springs. Head west from the circle, then north on Ocotillo Drive and Lazy S Drive. "Winter homes," the counterpart of the usual summer homes of most resort areas, dot the desert landscape. Come summer, there's a big exodus from the valley, leaving only a couple thousand or so permanent residents to hold

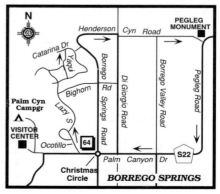

Trip 64

down the fort through the summer months. Borrego Valley's climate is similar to that of Palm Springs, with scorching summer highs of well over 100°, and winter highs in the 70s.

Follow Pointing Rock Drive, Yaqui Road, and Catarina Drive through and around the De Anza Country Club—Borrego's answer to the more elaborate golf courses of Palm Springs. The tortured, coppery escarpment of Indianhead Mountain rises to the west, starkly contrasting with the cool hues of manicured greens and fairways, and gracefully swaying palms. Borrego Valley is completely surrounded by the 650,000-acre Anza-Borrego Desert State Park, thus development for housing, tourism and agriculture will always be somewhat limited here.

Follow Santa Rosa Road to Borrego Springs Road and Henderson Canyon

Road. You now enter what is mostly an untouched desert landscape, interrupted occasionally by citrus orchards and groves of cultivated palms. If rainfall and sunshine have been timely enough, you'll find abundant displays of desert sunflower, dune primrose, and sand verbena. Fragrant tamarisk trees, planted as windbreaks along the roadsides, provide a measure of shade.

Next stop is Pegleg Monument, nestled against the south spur of Coyote Mountain. The marker commemorates Pegleg Smith, a prospector and spinner of tall tales, and his famous legend of lost gold. Adding stones to the big rock pile nearby, so it is said, brings luck to the treasure hunter.

You now return to Christmas Circle by going south on Pegleg Road and west on Palm Canyon Drive. A few miles east of Pegleg Road, mostly hidden from

Cholla cactus

view, are the Borrego Badlands. These desolate, dry creek beds, steep cliffs and ravines are almost completely devoid of plant life. Many an early prospector, so the stories tell, disappeared in these sandy wastes.

Options: Anza-Borrego Desert State Park's Visitor Center is located two miles west of Christmas Circle on Palm Canyon Drive. During the wildflower sea-

son, information about the best viewing areas is available here.

North of the Visitor Center, about two miles away by road, is the Borrego Palm Canyon Campground. This is the starting point of a popular foot trail to the groves of native palm trees in Borrego Palm Canyon. You can secure your bike at the trailhead, and then enjoy one of the best hiking trails in the California desert.

Trip 65. Coyote Canyon Classic

Starting Point: Anza (Riverside County)
GPS: Lat/Long 33° 30' 3", 116° 37' 48";
UTM 11S 534362mE 3706672mN
Distance: 36 miles
Elevation Gain: 250 feet
Elevation Loss: 3400 feet
Riding Time: 5 hours
Road Conditions: Rough and rocky, or sandy, dirt roads; smooth, paved road at the end
Traffic Conditions: Light
Difficulty: ****
Equipment: Mountain bikes only

There's no mistake in the capsulized summary above. This point-to-point *downhill* ride rates four stars! Mark our words: This ride will test your skills,

strength and endurance. The route is similar to that of the Coyote Canyon Clunker Classic mountain-bike ride, once regarded as one of the most difficult biking events in southern California.

Large organized bike rides, such as the Clunker Classic, are no longer allowed here. That means you must set up your own logistics and go on your own. The drive between end and start points takes about 90 minutes—so a car shuttle is simply too time-consuming. It makes sense to involve a friend or friends who can drop you off at the start and later pick you up at the end.

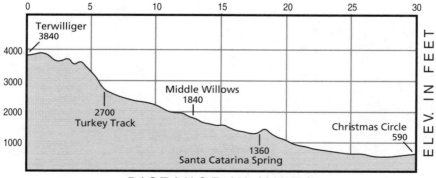

DISTANCE IN MILES

Middle Willows

It's nice to know that Coyote Canyon has never been invaded by a paved road, despite the fact that it serves as a topographically easy entrance into the desert from metropolitan southern California. This topography results because the canyon is underlain by a branch of the San Jacinto Fault, itself an offshoot of the San Andreas. The earliest expeditions by the Spaniards took advantage of this natural corridor: first in 1772 by Pedro Fages who was chasing deserters from the San Diego presidio, then in 1774 and 1775 by Juan Bautista de Anza who brought settlers from Sonora, Mexico, into northern California.

To reach the starting point, use Highway 79 (either from Temecula or from Warner Springs) to reach Aguanga. At

Aguanga, turn north on Highway 371, which will take you to the sprawling community of Anza, about 15 miles away. At a point 16.2 miles from Aguanga, turn south on Kirby Road. Continue, making a forced dogleg turn, 4.6 miles to the intersection of Terwilliger Road and graded Coyote Canyon Road on the left.

Make sure you have all you need, including lots of water, repair items, and minimum survival gear, before you launch yourself into the wilderness. You're on your own once your transportation crew pulls away.

Ride east on Coyote Canyon Road 1.7 miles to a **T**-intersection, and turn right. The road through the rolling tableland ahead becomes rougher. Soon

Trip 65

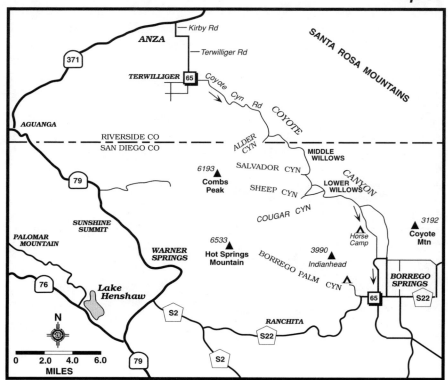

you get a view toward the rugged and lonely mountains of Cleveland National Forest to the west. Snow commonly dusts the higher elevations around here in winter, but you'll soon descend to a warmer clime.

At 3.5 miles, you climb a small, steep hill and reach the gated entrance to Anza-Borrego Desert State Park. The park authorities close the Coyote Canyon section to *all* visitors from the beginning of June through the end of September to protect the watering rights of the bighorn sheep. You'd be crazy to attempt this ride in the heat of summer anyway.

Soon a real downgrade begins. You won't do much sightseeing here—outside of about 10 feet from your nose. Though the road's been used as a primitive auto route for more than 60 years, little maintenance has been done on it for over a decade. Skilled riders will have a blast; semi-skilled riders should play it safe and walk down the worst of the rutted and rocky sections.

When you reach the bottom of the grade at Turkey Track, so named for the turkey-foot pattern of canyons that converge there, you'll meet the new challenge of soft sand. Unless it's recently rained and the sand is damp, we recommend letting some air out of your tires to increase the size of the tires' footprints. Continue southeast, staying on the faint jeep road that snakes through the wash.

At 9.0 miles, a sign directs the way on a side road to Alder Canyon and Baily's Cabin, 1.8 miles away. But stay left on the main route, if you're going to conserve your energy.

At Middle Willows (12.5 miles), you'll find a trickle—or more—of water on the ground, palm trees, and clumps of thorny mesquite bushes. At times you

actually ride through the water. Continue following the wash until you reach a signed junction—Monkey Hill Trail and Main Wash Trail. There's state wilderness land straight ahead, so bicyclists must follow the road swinging right toward the mouth of Salvador Canyon. This maneuver is a blessing in disguise, since once away from the wash you'll be on firmer ground. Stay left at the next two junctions, Salvador Canyon and Sheep Canyon, and return to the watercourse in Coyote Canyon at Santa Catarina Springs, 18.6 miles. Several oozing acres filled with lush vegetation comprise the springs. A historical marker on the hill to the south commemorates the passage of the Anza expeditions.

At Santa Catarina Springs, simply stay on the auto road, which climbs south. You pass near the historical marker, turn east, and then descend sharply back down to what is now the wet-all-year Coyote Creek just below Lower Willows at "Third Crossing." This seemingly awkward road detour out of the canyon was designed to shunt vehicles of all kinds away from the riparian, environmentally sensitive Lower Willows.

At 26.5 miles, you hit pavement at DiGiorgio Road. Follow this road 5.2 miles to Christmas Circle, the center of Borrego Springs. There you can accept the adulations of your transportation crew, and a cold beer or soda from the market across the street.

Trip 66. Borrego - San Felipe Loop

Starting Point: Borrego Springs
GPS: Lat/Long 33° 15' 24", 116° 22' 28";
UTM 11S 558299mE 3679694mN
Distance: 49.5 miles
Elevation Gain: 4400 feet
Riding Time: 5.5 hours
Road Conditions: Smooth roads with narrow to wide shoulders
Traffic Conditions: Light to moderate
Difficulty: ****
Equipment: Any multi-geared bike

Here's a ride that starts off with a real challenge—an unrelenting climb of 3600 feet. This is the longest sustained highway grade in San Diego County, and one that offers incredible views to boot. After the first 12 miles, you can simply let gravity repay you and coast down at least two-thirds of the remaining 38 miles.

An early start is recommended in order to avoid the broiling sun. We rode this ride in June, setting off in the predawn, 70-degree coolness and arriving at the Montezuma Highway summit an hour after sunrise. The heat wasn't a problem at all until the last dozen, mostly downhill miles.

To facilitate an early start in the morning, you can stay overnight at a

motel in Borrego Springs or camp out in any of Anza-Borrego Desert State Park's many developed and primitive campsites. You may want to (as we did) leave a water cache along Montezuma Highway as you drive in the day before the ride.

From Christmas Circle, you begin the climb immediately by going west on Palm Canyon Drive. After 1.4 miles, turn left on Montezuma Highway. Soon the gradient steepens, and then it stays at 5 percent to 8 percent grade for the next 10 miles. For several miles the highway twists back and forth along steep slopes adorned with stiff, thorny desert vegetation such as ocotillo, barrel cactus, cholla cactus and desert agave. In spring, the brittlebush (a low, dome-shaped shrub) shows off hundreds of daisy-like flowers. After a wet winter season, brittlebushes can paint entire hillsides a light shade of yellow.

As you climb, the view of Borrego Valley and its surrounding backdrop of mountains expand, and the Salton Sea comes into view 30 miles to the east. At the Crawford Overlook, 6.5 miles from Borrego Springs, there's a plaque that

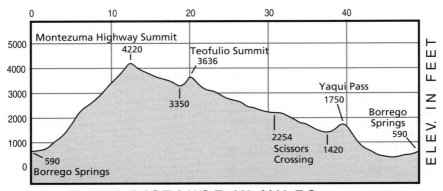

identifies the major peaks and other features on the horizon.

After Crawford Overlook, the road turns generally west and eventually enters the flatter terrain of Culp Valley. With an elevation of 2900-3400 feet, Culp Valley exhibits vegetation associated with the high desert—bright-green catclaw bushes; dark-green clumps of sugarbush and juniper; yucca; buckhorn cholla cactus; and various native grasses.

Ravens soar among the boulder piles heaped in the valley. A little higher still, the road crosses slopes clothed with thick, drought-resistant shrubs—very much like the chaparral country closer to the coast. A final steep pitch leads to the summit and the long-awaited relief from climbing.

Now you begin a long descent through Montezuma Valley, a gently sloping tableland dotted with a few small ranches and the homes of retirees. Water and other liquid refreshments are available at the small store in Ranchita, if it is open, but don't count on it.

When you reach San Felipe Road, turn left and begin a moderate climb through oak woodland to Teofulio Summit. Just beyond the pass is the tiny town of San Felipe, with its small store.

Highway 78 in Sentenac Canyon

With the usual prevailing winds blowing, you can average more than 20 miles per hour over the next few miles—just by coasting! In a few minutes you'll be back in a high desert environment. Look for the Pacific Crest Trail (hiking trail), which parallels this stretch of road for about 10 miles, up on the slope of the San Felipe Hills to your left. On the right are the dark, pine-crested Volcan Mountains.

At Scissors Crossing, turn left, following the bend of San Felipe Creek.

Soon the road begin a curving descent down Sentenac Canyon. You cross over the bubbling creek on a bridge; this is a good area to stop for a rest and a dip in the shallow water. The road then emerges from the mouth of the canyon and continues across open desert toward Tamarisk Grove Campground. You can obtain water at the campground for your final, short-but-grueling climb to Yaqui Pass.

Along the twisting roadway to Yaqui Pass, you can look down upon a vast,

Trips 66, 67

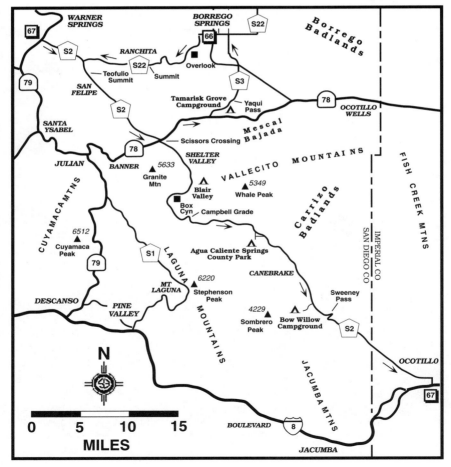

gently sloping plain to the south, bordered in the distance by the rugged Pinyon Mountains. It's called Mescal Bajada, after the desert agave (also called century plant or mescal) and the Spanish word *bajada*, which means more or less "sloping plain." From this vantage point you can easily visualize the effects of erosion on the nearby mountain ranges.

Beyond Yaqui Pass, your gaze takes in a magnificent panorama of Borrego Valley and the Santa Rosa Mountains. As you seemingly "come in for a landing" on the long downgrade to the valley floor, keep straight at the Borrego

Springs Road cutoff. Borrego Valley Road is a flatter and slightly shorter way to return to Christmas Circle.

Options: Consider expanding this loop to include Lake Henshaw, Santa Ysabel, and Julian for a complete desert-mountain tour, 72 miles in length. On a two-day trip, you could start in the desert and camp at a place like William Heise County Park near Julian (see the Julian Tour trip), or start at Santa Ysabel and make camp at one of Anza-Borrego's many campgrounds or primitive camping spots.

Trip 67. Old Emigrant Route

Starting Point: near Warner Springs
GPS: Lat/Long 33° 14' 58", 116° 40' 23"; UTM 11S 530451mE 3678788mN
Finish Point: Ocotillo
Distance: 64.5 miles
Elevation Gain: 1850 feet
Elevation Loss: 4300 feet
Riding Time: 5 hours
Road Conditions: Smooth roads with mostly wide shoulders
Traffic Conditions: Light
Difficulty: ***
Equipment: Any multi-geared bike

Known variously as the Carrizo Corridor, the Southern Emigrant Trail, and the route of the Butterfield Overland Mail, this natural pathway between the harsh desert floor and the cooler mountains played an important historical role in the 1800s. In the early 1950s a poor dirt road traced its course. Today, an asphalt ribbon, known as Highway S2, runs the length of the corridor, providing easy access to what was some 140 years ago a dreaded passage for emigrants.

You can't enjoy bicycling as carefree as this in many other places. Highway S2 is never busy and usually has a smooth, wide shoulder. The scenery ranges from bucolic to desolate, but you're never out of touch with the unique feeling of the open road.

The trip is best done as a point-to-point ride—northwest to southeast. This takes advantage of both a net loss of elevation from start to finish, and prevailing winds from the northwest. You'll have to arrange a car-shuttle or a drop-off-and-pick-up arrangement in order to do the trip one way. Any loop route incorporating all of Highway S2 is necessarily a very long one (see Grand Tours of the County, for ideas, in the Appendix).

Begin at the northwest terminus of Highway S2 at Highway 79, just south of Warner Springs. A gradual climb east takes you along the edge of a large valley chiefly used for cattle grazing. This

Blair Valley

is part of Valle de San Jose, a large depression that includes Lake Henshaw. To the north you'll see the pointed summit of Hot Springs Mountain (6533 feet)—highest elevation in San Diego County. Behind you is Palomar Mountain, with the conspicuous white dome of the 200-inch Hale Telescope in view.

Within the first mile, look on the left side of the road to see a barn with an adobe wall exposed. This is the remodeled remains of the Warner's Ranch station of the Butterfield Overland Mail, which was in operation for a short time around 1858. After about 4.5 miles, Highway S2 bends southeast and begins a sharper ascent through oak groves to Teofulio Summit. Just beyond the summit is a small store at the tiny town of San Felipe.

Ahead, a long downgrade takes you quickly through drier country country—Anza-Borrego's high desert. At Scissors Crossing (intersection of Highway 78),

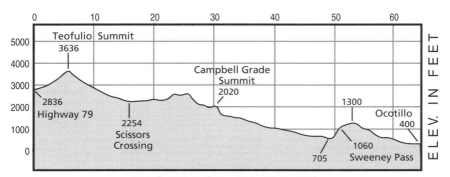

jog right, then left to remain on the S2 route. Earthquake Valley lies ahead with its private development of homes. Local real-estate agents would just as soon erase that name from the maps; they prefer to call it "Shelter Valley." A low summit is next, at a kink in the road. Beyond is beautiful Blair Valley, graced with thousands of desert agaves (century plants). In spring, the sight of thousands of yellow-flowered agave stalks across the valley can be quite amazing.

Soon the road takes a steep dive down Box Canyon, passing the spot where in 1847 members of the Mormon Battalion hacked away a passage for wagons through solid rock. Ahead, you emerge into gently sloping Mason Valley. You pass the Butterfield Ranch resort, and climb to another small summit. On the other side there's a deceptively steep downhill pitch—Campbell Grade. Take it slow and cautiously, lest you be catapulted onto the broken rock and cactus-infested slopes below.

After several more miles Vallecito County Park, with its restored Butterfield Overland Mail station, comes into view. You'll find picnic and camping facilities on the margin of a *cienaga*, or marshy area. After a few more miles, a paved side road leads to Agua Caliente County Park and the popular hot springs and pools. This is a mandatory stop whether the temperature is high or low. Even in hot weather, a dip in the warm water is refreshing. If you're camping along the way, this might be the place to stay.

From Agua Caliente on, Highway S2 stays within the domain of the low desert. Sand and cactus predominate now. Skeletal mountains rise in the west, and the sun beats down unmercifully most of the year. Even in this harsh landscape, though, there are spots of greenery on both sides of the road. Isolated mesquite and palm oases can be seen in the distance—Palm Spring, Mountain Palm Springs, and Bow Willow Palms. All are worth a visit if your bike is of the all-terrain variety.

At Sweeney Pass, the road goes sharply uphill for about a mile. Just past the road summit there's a turnout offering a panoramic view of the tortured Carrizo Badlands to the east.

A long, easy downgrade completes the ride. It can be especially fast if the usual prevailing winds are blowing squarely against your back. After five miles you cross the county line, entering Imperial County. After another five miles, you pull into the small desert town of Ocotillo. Here Highway S2 comes to a junction with Interstate 8, and you come to the end of a not-too-taxing and memorable ride.

Appendix 1. Getting Out of San Diego

Here we present information about getting out of (or into) San Diego using the most direct routes. These routes follow the natural or logical corridors through San Diego County's varied and somewhat broken terrain, so it's not surprising that you will be paralleling interstate freeways much of the time.

Occasionally you'll be forced to ride on the freeway shoulders themselves, for lack of any frontage roads or reasonable alternate routes. This is legal in California and in other states where these circumstances exist. If there is no sign at a freeway entrance ramp specifically prohibiting bicycles, then bicycle traffic is allowed. Once you're on a "legal" stretch of freeway, you'll be advised by a BICYCLES MUST EXIT sign where to get off.

The free San Diego Regional Bicycling Map (see Appendix 3) is very helpful for trans-county trip planning. In addition to hundreds of miles of suggested routes, it shows all segments of freeway open to bicycles within the San Diego metropolitan area. The following descriptions are best followed with the aid of either that map, the Thomas Brothers San Diego County atlas, or the San Diego county and street maps issued free to members of the Automobile Club of Southern California.

North Along the Coast

Several routes from various parts of San Diego converge near the Interstate 5/Interstate 8 interchange near Mission Bay. This includes routes parallel to I-5 from downtown San Diego, routes from Point Loma, and routes from both sides of Mission Valley. So we'll assume the I-5/I-8 interchange is where you begin your trip north.

The fastest way north is on Morena Boulevard, parallel to and east of I-5. Proceed about three miles north to the Balboa Avenue/Garnet Avenue crossing. Take the west-bound ramp (a cloverleaf) toward Garnet, but turn right immediately onto Santa Fe Street, heading north again. [If traveling southbound, it is better to follow this alternate route: From southbound Santa Fe Street, turn right on Damon Avenue; this leads to Mission Bay Drive. Turn left (south) on Mission Bay Drive and pedal south for about one mile. Just before the southbound lanes of Mission Bay Drive feed onto I-5, turn right at the traffic light to reach East Mission Bay Drive. Follow this along the east shore of Mission Bay (west of I-5) to Sea World Drive. Turn right there and then immediately left to cross I-5 and reach Pacific Highway, which passes under the I-5/I-8 interchange.]

Go north on Santa Fe Street, which dead ends ahead. You continue on the paved bike path paralleling I-5. The bike path ends at Gilman Drive. Go left and follow Gilman to the overpass at La Jolla Village Drive. Turn left onto the west-bound ramp and follow La Jolla Village Drive and North Torrey Pines Road around the west edge of the UCSD campus. At the point where Genesee Avenue continues east, it's necessary to make a left turn to stay on North Torrey Pines Road.

From now on, until you reach Oceanside about 23 miles away, you will be on the old coast highway, unofficially known as "Old Highway 101." Although it was relieved of heavy traffic by the completion of Interstate 5 around 1965, it still accommodates quite a bit of local traffic. Striped bike lanes accompany the route most of the way. Except for the long Torrey Pines grade on North Torrey Pines Road, and moderate grades north and south of Del Mar, the terrain is mostly flat. You get nice view of the Pacific Ocean occasionally, and there's always a fresh breeze blowing off the water.

As you pass through the string of North County beach towns, you can sometimes wend your way through pleasant residential areas by paralleling the highway one or two blocks away (see the North County Coast trip in this book for details).

In Oceanside, you can avoid busy Hill Street and enjoy some nicer scenery if you jog west on Cassidy Street several blocks to Pacific Street. After going north on Pacific Street for about two miles, turn right at 6th Street and return to Hill Street. Hill Street ends at Oceanside Harbor Drive. Turn right there, pass under I-5, and pedal up to the Camp Pendleton main gate. The route from this point up to the Orange County line at San Clemente is described in the Camp Pendleton Coast trip.

North Along Interstate 15

In this description, we assume you begin at the San Diego Stadium, adjacent to Interstates 8 and 15 in the middle of Mission Valley. From the northeast corner of the stadium parking lot, pick up the bike path that leads north under Friars Road along the west side of I-15. This path soon veers over the concrete top of a box culvert and follows it for some distance.

Leaving the culvert, the path joins the two-lane Murphy Canyon Road,

which has become a frontage road of the Interstate 15 freeway. After about three miles, Murphy Canyon Road intersects Clairemont Mesa Boulevard. Turn left, go two blocks, and turn right on Ruffin Road. Proceed north on Ruffin Road about one mile to where Kearny Villa Road joins from the left (make no turns).

Follow Kearny Villa Road north over Freeway 163. Nearly three miles of the old freeway (now renamed Kearny Villa Road) through Miramar Naval Air Station lie ahead, striped with wide bike lanes. The Interstate 15 freeway lies to the east.

Next, Kearny Villa Road swings northwest, crosses Miramar Road, and joins with Black Mountain Road. Continue north on Black Mountain Road for about 1.5 miles, then turn right (east) on Mira Mesa Boulevard. After crossing under I-15, turn left on Scripps Ranch Road. After one block, turn left (west) on Erma Road, which after another block bends right to parallel the freeway.

Erma Road soon ends, but a bike path continues, taking you alongside the northbound lanes of I-15 through a low pass. The path crosses Scripps-Poway Parkway and descends quite steeply to cross Los Penasquitos Creek on a picturesque concrete bridge that used to be a part of the main highway. The path now climbs to Poway Road.

Although bicycles are permitted on most of Interstate 15 from Poway Road north to Rancho Bernardo, here's a better route preferred by most cyclists: Go east on Poway Road 2.5 miles to Pomerado Road, and then north on Pomerado Road for 7.5 miles to I-15 north of Rancho Bernardo. Most of Pomerado Road is striped with bike lanes.

At I-15, take the northbound ramp and ride north across an arm of Lake Hodges. Exit at the next ramp (Via Rancho Parkway). When you come up to the traffic signal, use the WALK-DON'T WALK button to cross over to the northbound on-ramp of I-15. This is essentially a 180° turn. [For southbound cyclists, the maneuver is similar: exit I-15 and reenter southbound at Via Rancho Parkway.] You're back on I-15 for a short time. Exit at Centre City Parkway; this used to be the main highway through the middle of Escondido.

From now on, there are no turns for about 20 miles. After leaving central Escondido, Center City Parkway becomes the old two-lane Highway 395, now a frontage road of I-15. At the Mission Road exit for Fallbrook, go east over I-15 to join the frontage road on the other side. A few miles farther, in the Rainbow area, the route passes into Riverside County (see the Rainbow-Pala Loop trip).

Northeast to Julian and Borrego

For the strong bicyclist, San Diego County's backcountry areas are but a few hours away from any part of the San Diego metropolitan area. Here we describe the easiest routes to the unofficial capital of the county's high mountain area, Julian, and the unofficial capital of our local desert, Borrego Springs.

From central San Diego, first work your way over the city streets to Santee and Lakeside. The multi-laned Mission Gorge Road is a direct way to do this, although it is often busy with fast-moving traffic. West of Santee, you can avoid a big hill on Mission Gorge Road by taking a two-mile detour on Father Junipero Serra Trail (a two-lane paved road). This rather level alternate route follows the San Diego River through the impressive Mission Gorge.

After following Woodside Avenue (the frontage road along Freeway 67) into Lakeside, take Ashwood Street north to reach Wildcat Canyon Road. Although steep, the route north on Wildcat Canyon Road may be a better choice than the busier Highway 67. Note, however, that the expanded Barona Casino has increased traffic substantially on Wildcat Canyon Road.

Wildcat Canyon Road rises quickly to a summit, and then descends into the Barona Indian Reservation. After several miles of minor ups and downs, the road drops very suddenly and steeply to San Vicente Road. Turn left there, and go uphill (west, then north) over a summit. Continue riding north into the sprawling rural community of Ramona. After joining Highway 78 briefly (going northeast down Ramona's main street), turn right on 3rd Street. Third Street soon becomes the delightful Old Julian Highway, an alternative to Highway 78 that is actually shorter than the main highway, but with more turns. [At San Vicente Road, you can also go east and wend your way through the residential streets of San Diego Country Estates to reach Vista Ramona Road. On Vista Ramona you go up a steep grade and down to Old Julian Highway at a point two miles east of Ramona. This is an equally difficult alternative, but you would miss the facilities available in Ramona's town center.]

After seven miles of mostly gradual climbing on Old Julian Highway, you come back to Highway 78. Seven more miles of ups and downs on eastbound 78 take you to the Highway 79 junction and the crossroads community of Santa Ysabel.

East of Santa Ysabel, Highway 78/79 climbs seven miles to Julian (elevation 4200 feet—the high point on your trip). At Julian, Highway 79 goes south through the Cuyamaca Mountains to reach Interstate 8. You could continue east on 78, dropping down through Banner Canyon, if you wanted to reach the middle section of Anza-Borrego Desert State Park.

North of Santa Ysabel, Highway 79 leads north toward Lake Henshaw. At a point 11 miles north of Santa Ysabel, Highway S2 leads east toward Borrego Springs. One more turn is necessary: turn left on Highway S22, 4 miles ahead. The last 10 miles into Borrego Springs are entirely downhill, with an elevation loss of nearly 4000 feet. Your brakes must be in faultless working order!

East Along Interstate 8

A variety of routes on San Diego's city streets can take you east, paralleling Interstate 8. From central San Diego, pedal east, either on or parallel to El Cajon Boulevard or University Avenue, through East San Diego. At La Mesa, turn north on Baltimore Drive, cross over I-8, and then turn right (east) on Fletcher Parkway. Follow Fletcher Parkway two miles to Amaya Drive. Turn right, continue for about 0.5 mile, then bear right on Water Street. Water Street ends at Murray Drive, atop Grossmont Summit. Turn left on Murray and continue east, staying right at the next intersection under I-8 to El Cajon Boulevard in El Cajon.

El Cajon Boulevard soon merges into Main Street. Continue east through El Cajon's city center (or you can turn north to reach Madison Avenue, a parallel route with less traffic that eventually

comes back to Main Street.) At the east edge of El Cajon, Main Street passes under I-8 and continues northeast, generally parallel to and north of I-8. It is now called Old Highway 80 (or Highway 8 Business Route). You're now beginning a long ascent toward the mountains, which will be interrupted by only a few modest downgrades along the way.

When you reach Lake Jennings Park Road, turn right, cross under I-8, and pick up the Old Highway 80 frontage road on the south side of I-8. After about two miles, the old highway passes under I-8 and continues along the north side of I-8 to Dunbar Lane. Turn right, cross under I-8, and again pick up the old highway, now called Alpine Boulevard.

Alpine Boulevard descends sharply, then climbs steadily toward the town of Alpine (elevation 1700 feet). Continue straight ahead, staying on the south side of I-8 for another five miles. At East Willows Road, the frontage road comes to an end. You now continue on the eight-foot-wide shoulder of I-8.

After three miles on the freeway, you must exit at Highway 79/Japatul Road. Take 79 north past Descanso, then take Old Highway 80 up to Guatay, where you attain a 4000-foot summit. You then drop steeply down to Pine Valley, a good resting spot with plenty of facilities.

A short, steep grade leads from Pine Valley up to Sunrise Highway (Laguna Summit—4050 feet), where you cross over to the south side of I-8 and continue on the old highway roadbed.

For the next 30 miles, Old Highway 80 stays south of I-8, undulating between elevations of 2800 feet and 4200 feet. It passes through a series of small communities: notably Live Oak Springs, Boulevard and Jacumba. At Jacumba the highway comes to within a half mile of the Mexican border.

Beyond Jacumba, the mountains fall sharply away, and the desert floor lies below. Again you must take the only feasible route—the shoulder of I-8—down the 10-mile stretch known as the Mountain Springs grade. Usually this is a fast and enjoyable 2500-foot descent, but strong, shifting winds occasionally make this a hazardous stretch for bicyclists and autos alike. [These winds, prevailing from the west, can be impossible to fight if you're heading back uphill toward San Diego.]

There are two exits at the bottom of the grade. Take the first—Highway 98—if you're going on to Imperial Valley or Arizona. Take the second—Highway S2/Ocotillo—if you're going to head northwest into Anza-Borrego Desert.

Appendix 2. Grand Tours of the County

During a three- or four-day bicycle trip around San Diego County, a rider can see more varieties of natural terrain and vegetation than he or she would see on a trip lasting three or four weeks in most other parts of the United States. Here are two "grand tours" taking maximum advantage of San Diego County's extraordinary range of environments.

A Loop Through the Mountains

Beginning along the coast at San Diego and traversing the forested heights of both the Palomar and the Laguna mountains, this three-day, roughly 200-mile-long tour includes the highest paved highways in San Diego County. Best times are April through November. Pack your camping equipment along, or get someone with a car to haul your overnight gear up to the mountains.

Day 1: After riding north to Del Mar along the coast or parallel to Interstate 5, turn inland at the Del Mar fairgrounds/racetrack and continue east on Via de la Valle (Highway S6). Beyond Rancho Santa Fe, Highway S6 (now called Del Dios Highway) passes Lake Hodges and enters Escondido. Stay on S6 (Valley Parkway) through Escondido, and continue up Valley Center Road to Valley Center.

A few miles beyond Valley Center, S6 drops down to join Highway 76 at the foot of Palomar Mountain. Go east there, beginning the long climb to the top of the forested ridge above. After five miles, veer left to stay on Highway S6—now called South Grade Road. You reach the summit after seven more miles. Lodging is limited in the Palomar Mountain area, but several public campgrounds (some seasonal) are located a short distance away. Reservations may be required in summer and on busy weekends (see Appendix 3). If time allows, visit Palomar Observatory and Palomar Mountain State Park (see the Palomar Mountain Tour).

Day 2: Descend Palomar Mountain on East Grade Road, and arrive at Highway 76 near Lake Henshaw. Ride east on 76 to Highway 79, then go south over a pass to Santa Ysabel. From there, continue east on Highway 78/79 to Julian (see the Julian Tour).

After passing through Julian's town center, turn south on Highway 79 and go six miles toward Cuyamaca Reservoir. Turn left on Sunrise Highway (S1) and begin a long, undulating climb to the top of the Laguna Mountains. There's limited lodging in the resort village of Mount Laguna, but camping opportunities abound in the surrounding national forest. In addition to Laguna Campground (open all year), Burnt Rancheria Campground (seasonal), and a number of special purpose campgrounds, "remote camping" is allowed on certain national forest lands in the Lagunas on a free permit basis (see Appendix 3).

Day 3: A fast descent down Sunrise Highway brings you to Pine Valley. From there, it's mostly downhill along Interstate 8 into El Cajon and San Diego via Old Highway 80 (see Appendix 1—East Along Interstate 8).

A Loop Through the Desert

This trip begins and ends in El Cajon, east of San Diego. Included on this five-day, roughly 250-mile route is a rather complete tour of the paved roads within the half-million-acre Anza-Borrego Desert State Park, plus a concluding run through the forested country of the Cuyamaca Mountains. Best times are March-April and October-November—periods during which temperatures are neither too warm in the desert nor too cold in the mountains. Plan to camp out along the way at least part of the time. Either carry your camping gear, or rely on someone with a car to transport it for you.

Day 1: Go south a few miles from El Cajon, and follow Highway 94 east to Jamul (or use the alternate route to Jamul via Jamul Drive as in the Lyons Valley - Japatul Loop trip). Continue east

on Highway 94 through scenic hills and valleys toward Campo. The first night's camp can be at Potrero County Park (north of Potrero, just past the Tecate, Mexico turnoff), or at Lake Morena County Park, five miles north of Highway 94 at Cameron Corners.

Day 2: Continue east on Highway 94, joining Old Highway 80 at Boulevard. Follow Old 80 east through Jacumba, then ride on the shoulder of Interstate 8 down onto the desert floor at Ocotillo (see Appendix 1—East Along Interstate 8). From Ocotillo, begin a 50-mile-long trek northwest on Highway S2 (see the Old Emigrant Route trip) through the south half of the Anza-Borrego Desert State Park. Plan to camp somewhere along this road, either in one of the established campgrounds (Bow Willow, Agua Caliente, Vallecito, or Blair Valley) or anywhere along the roadside within the boundary of the state park (backcountry camping is permitted).

Day 3: Arriving at Scissors Crossing (Highway 78), turn east, descend through Sentenac Canyon, then turn north on Yaqui Pass Road. Once over Yaqui Pass, you drop down to the floor of Borrego Valley. Lodging is plentiful in the town of Borrego Springs, but you can also camp at nearby Borrego Palm Canyon Campground (reservations required here during the spring season). If time allows, you can explore more of the Borrego Valley area (see the Borrego Valley Desert Ride).

Day 4: Get an early start for the long, steep climb up Montezuma Highway (see the Borrego-San Felipe Loop trip). Five miles beyond the top, turn left on

Highway S2, climb to a summit, and then descend to reach Scissors Crossing again. There, turn right and tackle the twisting Banner Grade leading west up to Julian. Now turn south, ride past the shore of Cuyamaca Reservoir, and enter Cuyamaca Rancho State Park. Here in the shade of oaks and pines, you can stay at either Paso Picacho Campground or Green Valley Campground (reservations are needed on busy weekends).

Day 5: The last day is an easy one—almost entirely a downhill run. Continue south on Highway 79, then follow Interstate 8 and Old Highway 80 back to El Cajon (see Appendix 1—East Along Interstate 8).

Appendix 3. Resources and Recommended Reading

BICYCLE ORGANIZATIONS

For an up-to-date list of all bicycling clubs and organizations in San Diego County, pick up a copy of *Bicycling San Diego*, a free publication that is available at many bicycle and sports shops or visit their web site at www.bicyclingsandiego.com. Two organizations worth noting are the American Youth Hostels (AYH) and the San Diego County Bicycle Coalition (addresses and web site information below). These two organizations are committed to the improvement of bicycle facilities in the San Diego area. The AYH also sponsors local, national, and international bicycle trips, and operates hostels (low-cost lodging facilities for adventure travelers) in downtown San Diego and Point Loma.

The San Diego Chapter Sierra Club bicycle section sponsors several trips weekly. The monthly ride list is available via the Internet at www.sandiego.sierraclub.org/bicycle

EVENTS

Bicycling San Diego and a number of other periodicals publish lists of local bicycling events for the upcoming months. Some of the other titles include *Southern California Bicyclist*, *Southern California Bicycling*, and *Race Place San Diego*. These free publications are available at bicycle shops as well as many athletic shoe stores.

MAPS

Good maps are useful companions to this book, and are essential for planning long trips. The free *San Diego Regional Bicycling Map*, available from CalTrans, outlines hundreds of miles of suggested routes in the built-up areas of the county, but by no means exhausts all possibilities.

The best coverage of the remainder of the county is the Automobile Club of Southern California's San Diego County map; this map plus four useful city street maps covering the urban parts of the county are available to club members. The annually updated *Thomas Brothers San Diego County Street Guide and Directory*, available at most bookstores, covers the entire county. The county's foothills, mountains, and part of the desert is well-covered on the Cleveland National Forest recreation map.

Serious cyclists may want to consult the large-scale U.S. Geological Survey topographic maps; these are available in the county at Map World, Map Centre, Adventure 16 Wilderness Outfitters (A16), and Recreational Equipment, Inc. (REI). See below for address and web site information.

GPS STARTING POINTS

Each ride now includes the GPS co-ordinates of its starting point. These co-ordinates appear in latitude and longitude format and in UTM (Universal Transverse Mercator) format. These points were determined using National Geographic's TOPO!GPS program using the North American 27 Datum (NAD27) which is currently used on most USGS topographic maps. Make sure you set your GPS options to the NAD27 datum and either latitude/longitude (degrees, minutes, seconds) or the UTM coordinate system. If you would like more information about GPS and co-ordinate systems, visit these Internet sites:
http://www.maptools.com/UsingUTM/index.html
http://www.garmin.com/aboutGPS/manual.html
http://www.howstuffworks.com/gps.htm

PUBLIC TRANSPORTATION

With the abundance of bicycle-hauling services offered by local public transit companies, it is feasible to plan a variety of one-way trips throughout the cities and backcountry areas of San Diego County.

Bicycle rack service (at no extra charge) is available on all North County Transit District bus routes.

San Diego Transit offers a free brochure detailing certain routes and how to use the bus bike racks.

The San Diego Trolley now accepts bicycles (during certain hours) on its runs from downtown San Diego to El Cajon and to the international border. A permit is no longer necessary for this service.

The mini-vans of the Northeast Rural Bus System, providing service from El Cajon to the backcountry communities of Warner Springs, Julian, Borrego Springs and Agua Caliente, will take bicycles aboard on weekdays.

The Coaster commuter trains running between Oceanside and downtown San Diego also welcome cyclists, whose bikes can be easily secured in any of the rail cars. Stops include the Santa Fe Depot, Old Town, Solana Beach, Encinitas, Carlsbad Poinsettia, Carlsbad Village, and Oceanside.

Finally, bicycles may be taken aboard the Amtrak Surfliner trains between downtown San Diego and Los Angeles. Stops include Solana Beach, Oceanside, and San Clemente.

FOR MORE INFORMATION

- San Diego County Bicycle Coalition, P.O. Box 34544, San Diego, CA 92163, 858-487-6063. Web page: www.sdcbc.org
- American Youth Hostels, San Diego Council, 437 J Street, Suite #315, San Diego, CA 92101 619-338-9981. Web page: http://www.hiayh.org/home.shtml
- Sierra Club, San Diego Chapter, 3820 Ray Street, San Diego 92104, 619-299-1743. Web page: http://sandiego.sierraclub.org

- San Diego Regional Transit Telephone Information (for all carriers) 619-233-3004. Direct line for trip planning for buses, trolleys, and the Coaster. Web page: http://www.sdcommute.com
- California Department of Transportation (CalTrans) call 619-231-BIKE (2453) for bike information or to order a San Diego County Bike Map. Order a map online at www.ridelink.org/bicycle.html
- The San Diego County Transit System provides local bus services linking many cities in East San Diego County. They also provide transportation services connecting the Northeast & Southeast rural areas of San Diego County with El Cajon, La Mesa and Escondido. Call 760-767-4BUS (4287) or visit their web page: http://www.co.san-diego.ca.us/cts
- Amtrak, 800-872-7245. Web page: http://www.amtrakcalifornia.com
- Cleveland National Forest camping information, 858-673-6180. Web page: http://www.r5.fs.fed.us/cleveland
- California State Parks camping information, 800-444-PARK (7275). Web page: http://www.cal-parks.ca.gov
- San Diego County Parks camping information, 877-565-3600. Web page: http://www.co.san-diego.ca.us/cnty/cntydepts/landuse/parks
- Automobile Club of Southern California, 619-233-1000. Web page: http://www.aaa-calif.com
- Map World, 123-D North El Camino Real, Encinitas, 760-942-9642. Web page: www.mapworld.com
- Map Centre, 3191 Sports Arena Blvd., Suite F, San Diego, 619-291-3830. Web page: www.mapworld.com

- Recreational Equipment, Inc. (REI), 5556 Copley Drive, San Diego, 858-279-4400. Web page: www.rei.com
- Adventure 16 Wilderness Outfitters, 4620 Alvarado Canyon Road, San Diego, 619-283-2374. Web page: http://www.adventure16.com
- San Dieguito River Park information, www.sdrp.org, 858-674-2270. Volunteers are always needed to help with trail maintenance.
- San Marcos trail information, http://www.ci.san-marcos.ca.us/cs/trails/mainframe.html
- Daley Ranch trail information, http://www.ci.escondido.ca.us
- Mission Trails Regional Park information, http://www.mtrp.org
- Anza-Borrego Desert State Park information, 760-767-5311. Web page: http://www.anzaborrego.statepark.org/

RECOMMENDED READING

- *Afoot and Afield in San Diego County*, Jerry Schad, Wilderness Press, 1998
- *Anybody's Bike Book*, Tom Cuthbertson, Ten Speed Press, 1998
- *Anza-Borrego Desert Region*, 4th ed., Lowell and Diana Lindsay, Wilderness Press, 1998.
- *Effective Cycling*, John Forester, MIT Press, 1993
- *San Diego!...City and County*, Carol Mendel, 1990
- *San Diego Mountain Bike Guide*, Daniel Greenstadt, Sunbelt Publications, 1998
- *Sloane's Complete Book of All-Terrain Bicycles*, Eugene Sloane, Simon and Schuster, 1991
- *Walking San Diego: Where to Go to Get Away From it All*, Lonnie Hewitt and Barbara Moore, The Mountaineers, 2000

Index

SUNBELT PUBLICATIONS

"Adventures in the Natural and Cultural History of the Californias"

General Editor—Lowell Lindsay

Southern California Series:

Geology Terms in English and Spanish	Aurand
Portrait of Paloma: A Novel	Crosby
Orange County: A Photographic Collection	Hemphill
California's El Camino Real and its Historic Bells	Kurillo
Mission Memoirs: Reflections on California's Past	Ruscin
Warbird Watcher's Guide to the Southern California Skies	Smith
Campgrounds of Santa Barbara and Ventura Counties	Tyler
Campgrounds of Los Angeles and Orange Counties	Tyler

California Desert Series:

Anza-Borrego A to Z: People, Places, and Things	D. Lindsay
The Anza-Borrego Desert Region (Wilderness Press)	L. and D. Lindsay
Geology of the Imperial/Mexicali Valleys (SDAG 1998)	L. Lindsay, ed.
Palm Springs Oasis: A Photographic Essay	Lawson
Desert Lore of Southern California, 2nd Ed.	Pepper
Peaks, Palms, and Picnics: Journeys in Coachella Valley	Pyle
Geology of Anza-Borrego: Edge of Creation	Remeika, Lindsay
California Desert Miracle: Parks and Wilderness	Wheat

Baja California Series:

The Other Side: Journeys in Baja California	Botello
Cave Paintings of Baja California, Rev. Ed.	Crosby
Backroad Baja: The Central Region	Higginbotham
Lost Cabos: The Way it Was (Lost Cabos Press)	Jackson
Journey with a Baja Burro	Mackintosh
Houses of Los Cabos (Amaroma)	Martinez, ed.
Mexicoland: Stories from Todos Santos	Mercer
Baja Legends: Historic Characters, Events, Locations	Niemann
Loreto, Baja California: First Capital (Tio Press)	O'Neil
Baja Outpost: The Guest Book from Patchen's Cabin	Patchen
Sea of Cortez Review	Redmond

San Diego Series:

Rise and Fall of San Diego: 150 Million Years	Abbott
Only in America	Alessio
More Adventures with Kids in San Diego	Botello, Paxton
Geology of San Diego: Journeys Through Time	Clifford, Bergen, Spear
Mission Trails Regional Park Map	Cook
Cycling San Diego, 3rd Edition	Copp, Schad
La Jolla: A Celebration of Its Past	Daly-Lipe
A Good Camp: Gold Mines of Julian and the Cuyamacas	Fetzer
A Year in the Cuyamacas	Fetzer
San Diego Mountain Bike Guide	Greenstadt
San Diego Specters: Ghosts, Poltergeists, Tales	Lamb
San Diego Padres, 1969-2002: A Complete History (Big League Press)	Papucci
San Diego: An Introduction to the Region (3rd Ed.)	Pryde
Campgrounds of San Diego County	Tyler